To Riki Latimer
with highest regards for
your work in the vineyard.

Ad Majorem Dei Gloriam

PARADISE COMMANDER

PARADISE COMMANDER

Albert E. Hughes, Lt Colonel USAF (Ret)

Paradise Commander

Designed by James Kent Ridley

Published by Goodbooks Media Mill

Printed in the United States of America

We praise God by recalling his marvelous deeds.
Cassiodorus

Ad Majorem Dei Gloriam

ISBN-13: 978-1480291553
ISBN-10: 1480291552

goodbook
GOODBOOKS MEDIA MILL

For
Shannon, Katie and Martha

In Thanksgiving
For the
Love, Justice, and Mercy
of the
Triune God

Dedication

To all who lived and worked in the Antiguan Paradise, 1977 – 1979
Especially
His Excellency Governor, Sir Wilfred and Lady Jacobs
British Government Representative, Ian and Vivien Thow
Honorable Premier, Vere Bird, Sr.
Doctor, Sir Luther and Lady Wynters
Secretary, External Affairs and Defense, Eric Challenger
Aerodrome Superintendent, Dennis Nanton
Pan Am Managers, Jim Edwards, Harry James and Al Von Levern
Commander, 2179th CIG, Colonel and Mrs. Blocker
Spouse, friend and protocol "officer," Gloria Jean "Jeannie" Hughes
Housemaid and friend, Dorset Lincoln
Taxi Driver Gomez, pronounced "Gumzee" in the Island.
And at Patrick AFB
Commander, Eastern Test Range, Colonel Oscar and Barbara Payne
Down Range Affairs, Jack Oakes and Jenny Bailey

Acknowledgement

Many have contributed to Paradise Commander directly and indirectly in their friendship and personal support, but in particular it was Ronda Chrevin, Ph.D. who, in her writers group at Our Lady of Corpus Christi, inspired and encouraged me to begin writing what became several chapters; "Jeannie" Hughes, my beloved spouse at my side who has been my spiritual guide all these years and who kept the pressure on me to write; and my good friend James Ridley (Ronda's recent publisher) who took my unadorned manuscript, added pictures and graphics, reformatted the whole work and turned it into a book. Finally, I urge you carefully to peruse the dedication page that identifies many others to whom I owe so much.

Albert E. Hughes, Lt Colonel, USAF (Ret); MS, MM

CONTENTS

PREAMBLE

Jeannie, my wife, often says, "God has a plan for everyone; God has a plan." She has been saying that all our married life. She has a lot of good company in that belief. From religious scholars to congregation back benchers, many active Christians believe it and will say it. "God has a plan for everyone." Our challenge is to discover and live according to that plan. But of course, for the first half of my life, all that made no sense to me.

I was un-churched from the beginning. As a child, the only time I saw the inside of a church was while visiting our small town middle-Mississippi Baptist relatives: maternal grandparents, aunts, uncles and cousins. My immediate family's church-going at Hazlehurst and only there was all a sham, perpetrated to keep up appearances for the relatives who feared the shame of small town gossip. It was no surprise that from the ripe old age of 14, I declared myself an agnostic. Nevertheless, a plan emerged: my plan!

At 21 I was commissioned a Second Lieutenant in the United States Air Force. At 26 I was a young Captain working at Cape Canaveral (and probably) the only active duty Air Force Captain anywhere living on a sailboat. To cut to the chase, I married the girl on the boat next door. Big family uproar! She was, and is, Catholic!

Houseboat

Courtship

At 36, still agnostic, I achieved a long term goal: I took command of Antigua Air Station, West Indies, in the far eastern Caribbean. As it turned out, we flew right into a never-to-be-repeated time of radical change for West Indies governments, politics and cultures. At the same time, it was there that God's plan overtook me. In retrospect, it must have been His plan all along; I just didn't know it in those early years.

I now will tell you this, only: when the Infinite One first speaks directly to you, it really gets your attention!

The book in your hand sets the stage and reveals, chapter by chapter, the steady unfolding of radical change; political and cultural conversion for the island peoples and religious conversion for me. Jeannie was right. He did have a plan for us all.

Albert E. Hughes, Lt Col, USAF (retired); MS, MM

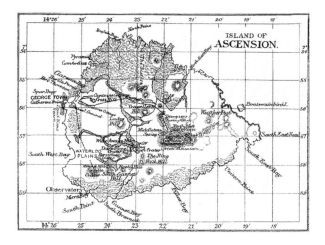

PROLOGUE: FOR LACK OF REIGN

Only mad dogs and Englishmen go out in the noon day sun.

Gilbert and Sullivan

Augustwas calm, beastly hot and cloudless at mid-Atlantic, just south of the equator. I stood in the mid-day glare alongside His Honor Brian Kendall, British Administrator of Ascension Island. We were fifty yards up the gravel road leading from the ocean wharf to Ascension Air Force Base. In the glare, through squinting eyes, the gravel road was barely discernible from the rock, sand and dust that covered the island. There was no vegetation to be seen except high up on Green Mountain, the extinct volcanic centerpiece of the island. We were returning from the wharf; a creosote black structure often washed clean by 30 foot rollers that occasionally broke over the deck. When rollers spawned by distant storms came in for two or three days at a time every few weeks, it was impossible to land ship or boat. Ships would anchor off and wait the better part of a week to off load supplies.

The wharf was new, but the warehouse at the side of the road was quite old. Implacable walls stood before us, massive sandstone blocks stacked and fitted stone upon stone in the ancient way, one hundred feet across the front and sixty feet down each side. The pale orange, yellow and tan sandstone blocks mimicked the gravel and the entire terrain, everything but the pale blue sky and the deep blue sea. "I have seen similar buildings and ruins all over the Eastern Caribbean, especially at Trinidad, Saint Lucia and in Antigua's English Harbor," I allowed.

"Of course, Major," Brian said. We stepped through the large center portal facing us. There was no door to close, no glass in two tiny windows at the far corners, no electric lights to reveal the contents. Our eyes adjusted slowly from outside glare to the dark, cool interior, revealing a tractor and a few implements in the far right corner. In the cave like comfort of warehouse shade, Brian continued. "Of course; I have seen them in India and East Africa as well, they are everywhere. It's quite simple. The architects of the British Empire were in England, in the Admiralty home office. They provided standard designs for the Empire's buildings. His Majesty's Navy and the colonists used local materials, but everywhere, the same designs."

He was looking up at ghostly shapes high overhead in the darkness, exposed ceiling beams revealed by sunlight peeking through random cracks and pin holes in the old roof. Massive beams, whole trees squared off by adz, hung suspended in slots atop the stone walls. They had been resting there for nearly 300 years. The warehouse was still in use, never mind the holes in the roof. It seldom rained except at the peak of Green Mountain.

"The Empire got its money's worth from this old warehouse!" I yelled.

Touchdown on Ascension's barren landscape

I doubt he heard me. An Air Force C-141 was passing low overhead in the landing pattern, turning toward final approach. Its four screaming jet engines were working loud against drag; flaps down, gear down, everything hanging in the breeze. It was arriving four hours late, southbound from Antigua Air Force Station in the West Indies. At dusk, it would lift Jeannie and me homeward, returning to Antigua by the following morning. We would travel and sleep all night in Air Force "first class," on pipe and olive drab canvas seats set up in front of the cargo pallets. But now, it was lunch time; we hurried up the road to join our wives at the club.

That C-141 was joining another on the ramp. The airplane originally scheduled to take us home was still sitting on the tarmac where we had deplaned from it four days previously; it was waiting spare parts shipped on today's southbound. Once repaired, it would continue to its turnaround at Pretoria, South Africa on the bi-monthly State Department run; returning through Ascension, Antigua, and Patrick AFB, Florida; then finally home to Charleston AFB.

USAF C-141 awaiting repairs

That flight delay for minor repairs extended our stay by two wonderful days, allowing a four day exploration of this rarely seen island. Ascension sits less than eight degrees below the equator at mid-Atlantic. There was no indigenous population there, only Ascension Air Base, a NASA station, British Cable and Wireless, and British administrative and support services, including the English version of a grade school for dependent children. Need a doctor? He visits monthly from England, or you may see the Pan Am medic at the air base.

Everyone present there was authorized by either the government of the United Kingdom or by the government of the United States. Nearly everyone arrived and departed by C-141, as did we. The British had two choices: fly commercial to Pretoria, SA and back track from there by USAF C-141 or fly British Airways direct to Antigua West Indies, thence to Ascension on a military flight. The gateway for US military and contractor employees was at Patrick AFB, Fla.

We were house guests of His Honor Brian and Jeanne Kendall---as gracious a pair of hosts as you could dream up in a Victorian novel. Their invitation to us was in return for the courtesies we had extended to them on occasion as they transited Antigua, including overnight stays at our house for their unaccompanied children en route to and from English boarding schools.

Halfway up Green Mountain

His Honor, the island Administrator, was a member of the British Foreign Service in official residence at Ascension. And what a residence! Their home had been a large, early 19th century stone built hospital; designed by Admiralty architects, of course. Converted, it had all the charm and staff services of a baronial manor. (The half dozen servants were from St Helena Island, 400 miles to the south. They attended to all residential needs.) Brian said more than once, "Her Majesty pays the Foreign Service in perks, not cash." The residence, on the lower slopes of Green Mountain, was just high enough to get a little water off the peak.

That water sustained an ancient garden of huge cactus plants, a great place to watch South Atlantic sunsets.

Green Mountain from afar
(Volcanic rock, not vegitation, in the foreground)

The day before our departure, we were driven up Green Mountain's narrow switchback road to Grenadiers' Walk. There, countless sentry footfalls left a dangerous, narrow dirt path cut into a steep, grass slick slope 200 feet below and all around the peak. A misstep there would reward you with a long, painful if not fatal slide down the cone shaped mountain! There, day and night, sentries had watched for French ships that might attempt to rescue Napoleon held in exile at St Helena. As we stood on that path, we could see a small, red hulled ship off the ocean wharf. It was newly arrived; the only passageway from England to Saint Helena, which had no airport. Anchored well off and far below our Green Mountain lookout, she was due to sail for St Helena the day after our departure. How I longed to be aboard!

There was not much to see from the south side except the endless waters of the South Atlantic. Below us though, in a water-capturing narrow notch near the bottom of the mountain, there was a most impressive stand of spruce; the only real trees on the island. They were planted to provide His Majesty's warships and merchantmen with replacement masts. There, these magnificent trees still watch the centuries pass by, straight, tall and proud; awaiting ships that will never sail.

Awaiting ships that will never sail

The sight of the little red-hulled ship and those trees waiting in vain for a call to duty touched a responsive chord. Our ancestry rests in the British Isles: English, Irish, Scots and Welsh. I grew up with my mother's teaching enthusiasm for English history, culture and language; with grand stories of imperial glory reinforced by Hollywood dramas and documentaries. Serving England's finest hour, Churchill was my early role model and hero.

From the destruction of the Spanish Armada to the defeat of the Nazis, the sun had not set on the world wide British Empire. But in the late nineteen seventies, the Empire was in its last days. Even then, in the twilight of imperial glory, we were able to discern in a very personal way the fascinating inner workings of the old British Empire at Ascension and especially at home in Antigua, West Indies.

The British were in final stages, shutting down colonies that remained in the Caribbean. They established their Caribbean colonies as a Federation of the West Indies. The Federation quickly failed. "The economically stronger islands did not want to carry the weak," I was told; but that was a simplification. As Emerson wrote, "The glory of friendship is not the out stretched hand, nor the kindly smile nor the joy of companionship; it is the spiritual inspiration that comes to one when he discovers that someone else believes in him and is willing to trust him."

The spiritual inspiration that comes from trust! Did the islanders of all the old Caribbean colonies - descendants of slaves- believe in themselves and trust in one other? Unspoken, but evident, many doubted so. Generations of slavery, more generations of economic servitude to the Empire had led to a deep sense of dependency upon the colonial masters: more trust in the English than in themselves. Can we really go independent? Can we be successful or will we sink into conflict, chaos and abject poverty? No belief in one another? *No spirit of unity.*

Everyone was a bit too leery of the other, especially island to island, but even to a certain extent village to village! Individually, the more economically sufficient Bahamas, Jamaica, Trinidad and Tabago, and Barbados went independent on their own, but smaller islands were not ready.

*

How to proceed? The British established Antigua and Barbuda, among others, as "States in Association with Great Britain." In effect, the Brits organized a school of independence and a test of readiness for seven small, relatively poor proto-nations.

In our time there Antiguans, in association with Great Britain, were independent in their internal affairs. They had an elected Parliament, a Premier, the usual government ministries, a police force, and an initial Defense Force Cadre. There were two established parties, Liberals and Conservatives, plus about 40 self-styled Marxists. The total island population was about 70,000; they were a rural county population raised to the national level! Another 70,000 Antiguans were scattered about in England, Canada and the United States. Ian Thow, the British Government Representative, acted as a hands-off advisor, best I ever could tell. The visible policy was, "Let the people work it out. Let them build a Nation for themselves."

The British continued to provide for external affairs and defense through His Excellency Governor, Sir Wilfred Jacobs, a barrister from Barbados appointed by Queen Elizabeth II. Ian Thow represented the executive government of Great Britain. Antigua had the full protection of the British Navy and Marines (who always seemed to sail to our warmer waters in mid-Winter.) Due to this interim form of government, Antigua Air Station flew three flags over the front gate; The United States of America, the United Kingdom of Great Britain, and the Associated State of Antigua and Barbuda.

Antigua Air Station was part of the Air Force Eastern Test Range, extending south-east from Cape Canaveral through five bases and stations at Grand Bahama, Grand Turk, Antigua, Ascension and Pretoria.

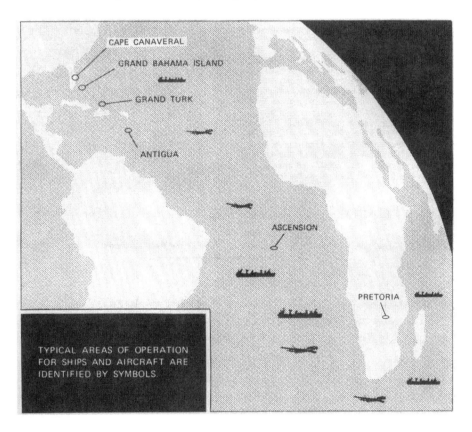

The Antigua airstrip and terminal had been ceded to the Antiguans, but we still conducted ground handling and loading of US military traffic: typically 30 plus aircraft and a few supply ships each month. The air strip also served British Airways, Eastern Airlines, Air Canada, and Leeward Island Air Transport (LIAT.) The station was managed by Pan Am World Airways; the missile and spacecraft tracking, telemetry and communications mission was conducted by their sub-contractor, RCA. Antiguans called (and pronounced) it "de Pahn Ahm Base!" The Base Commander was the only military assigned! What was he there to do?

Monitor Pan Am contract compliance to be sure; but also to administer the Status of Forces Agreement with Great Britain, conduct US Military Air and Sea Lift control and represent the US government to all government agencies and individuals operating on the island: usually US, British, Canadian, Antiguan, and Venezuelan.

Government representation turned out to be my principal task. Our nearest US Ambassador was at Barbados, way down south, so in day to day operations and liaison, I was the US government. I spent two years there as a quasi-diplomat. Tough duty! All that liaison with government agencies at the station, downtown in government ministry and agency offices, in many a cultural venue and so often at nightly cocktail parties all around the island, including the many we hosted at home. But that was how I kept my ear to the ground to know what really was going on; on the island, in the eastern Caribbean, where Castro's forces were probing and where I could strike and maintain functional alliances with certain Antiguan departments and agencies. Yes, the Major *was* the US government as far as other officials were concerned. I was busy up to 70 hours a week that first year, though officer friends in the US accused me of being on a two year paid vacation in my Caribbean Paradise.

We were there in the last days before Antigua's final liberation, participating first hand in the public life of a proto-nation as Antiguans of all levels struggled with the meaning of liberation and consequent responsibility; struggled to find their *Spirit of Unity.*

In the Associated State of Antigua and Barbuda, the meek were about to inherit the earth.

As I took command early morning on 28 June 1977, I had no way of knowing that I, too, was in my last days before liberation. I, too, would discover the meaning of true liberation and consequent responsibility; yes, and joy and awe and wonder, too. I, too, would find *The Spirit of Unity.*

I. Taking the Reins–June 1977

ANTIGUA WEST INDIES

Faithful friends are a sturdy shelter: whoever finds one has found a treasure. Faithful friends are beyond price; no amount can balance their worth. Faithful friends are life-saving medicine; and those who fear the Lord will find them.   Sirach 6:14-16 NRSV

In the Parish of Saint Mary trade winds lift precious moisture to the summit at Boggy Peak, releasing life giving rain in season. On Boggy's southern slopes the narrow road twists and turns through dense jungle around Fig Tree Hill, turning south to Carlyle Bay, then west along the beach to Johnsons Point, Crab Hill, and Valley Church. Here in the southwest corner of Antigua, a simple man can live off the island and want for nothing. Mangos and breadfruit, plantain, papaya and coconut grow wild and plentiful a short walk from the Caribbean sea. "Cas yo net off de beach, mon; have a leetle fish jus now. Tek a job? Jus now, mon. Osk me tomorrow. Ah tek a little res jus now, mon."

So it had been for living memory, but now the trees were dormant; the ponds dry, cracked mud. The few wells that worked at all were brackish and slack. "Yo gots to wuk haad fow to pomp a drink, mon, but ova dare, it mos wus." With a wave of the hand, "ova dare" was the rest of the island.

No cows, no crops, no relief, no life

In those days, we lived up in Hodges Bay, just east of Cedar Grove, along the Atlantic shore road two miles northwest of Antigua Air Station. Only nine by eighteen miles large, Antigua marks the northeast corner of the Caribbean: the Atlantic just across our road to the north and east, the Caribbean over the low hills behind us to the south and west. Characteristic of the Caribbean, Antigua is an island of easterly trade winds; of swaying palms, cheap rum and steel bands playing to tourists on moonlit beaches; land of a gentle, long suffering, but joyous people of quiet dignity; descendants of African slaves. At our arrival, it should have been a tropical paradise.

Instead, for years cotton ball clouds had surfed tropic winds close over the heads of a dwindling supply of tourists; brown palm leaves nodded and scraped a raspy cadence of the dying. First the northeast trades, then the southeast trades returned again in annual cycles marking the change of seasons year after year. The wet seasons were dry, the dry seasons desperate. "No rain jus now, mon. No rain on de lan, no rain on de wata, no rain on de mountain. Ah jus don know, mon; Ah jus don know."

It had gone on much too long. It wasn't that cows were dying in the fields over Parham Bay and Willikies; at Sweets, All Saints or Newfield: they were long dead of hunger and thirst. Bleached bones lay in parched fields on lunar dry hills. No cows, no crops, no money, no relief, no life.

Paradise Commander takes command

Nor was Harry happy. Rushing back from my incoming change of command ceremony; intent on some shop crisis, he had been summoned to the Base Manager's office to "Show the new major around." I noted condescension in the manager's voice, but let it pass. Harry's blue-black Brazilian face was all stony eyes and tight lips. A mechanical handshake and a mercy begging grimace at his boss told me this maintenance manager had no time for the major. The Base Manager insisted. I didn't need a tour, but neither he nor Harry knew how familiar I was with Antigua Air Station. At the very beginning of my first day, I was not going to start our relationship in conflict over a minor issue. I depended on the Base Manager to run a first class mission for the next two years.

In disgusted silence Harry led me up the low hill behind the office to the shops area, selected a dusty pickup truck from the motor pool, kicked the tires (one was low, which *really* increased his pique), waved me on board, pumped some gas, and fired up the engine. At the power house he executed a neck snapping right turn down the hill past the water treatment plant and roared out the main gate, turning right toward High Point pier and the east bound Atlantic beach road. This was going to be a record breaking, high speed new commander windshield tour!

Harry was not going to spoil my day. For years, I had dreamed of commanding this base, ever since first working there for two weeks as a young lieutenant. This warm June morning was going to accomplish a triumphal pleasure tour for me; but if Harry wanted to be miserable, I was ready to help. I began to pepper him with questions about *everything* we saw as he raced along.

"Where do we get the fresh water? How much chlorine do we use? How much water can we store? Is corrosion a problem in the salt water fire suppression and flushing system? Can the motor pool overhaul trucks? Can the carpenter shop handle major construction? What is the generating capacity of the power plant? Where do we get our diesel fuel? Was a crypto tech always on duty in the communications building? Were they Air Force trained? Is High Point pier restricted to our use only? Are those our power lines to the remote sites?

Harry was not moved by my show of interest. In response to a machine gun spray of questions, he spit fired single shots, yes or no; at long intervals he rewarded me with a short phrase. Raging non-verbal's proclaimed his impatience with the ignorant major. For a blue-black Brazilian, his knuckles certainly were turning pale on that steering wheel.

Quickly, we arrived at the telemetry site atop a low hill overlooking Long Island and the Atlantic. Overhead, the massive antenna dish, 80 feet in diameter, 100 odd feet in the air, was at horizontal rest.

TAA– 8A Telemetry Antenna

It resembled a flying saucer at dock. (Years earlier, as a young Air Force engineer, I participated in the source selection of Philco-Ford to design and build it.) My knowledge of it presented a great opportunity to pepper Harry with more questions. We dismounted at the concrete block operations building for an inside tour, then drove on to the space tracking radar over behind the LIAT hangars. Its 16 foot diameter dish hung mast high next to another concrete block building in a cluster of rusty, dusty Quonset huts and dead brown palmettos. Respectively, red and blue flashing lights indicated danger; the big dish could move suddenly in a snap shift and it was transmitting 5 megawatts, a deadly beam at close range. Harry phoned in and the lights went out, first the blue, then the red. We entered the site.

At both the telemetry and radar site, the routine was the same. Harry introduced me to the lead tech, who introduced me to his crew. After what goes for pleasantries in manly technical circles, (but not Harry's pleasantries to be sure) the lead techs led me through mind numbing tours of countless electronic racks and cabinets, explaining the function of each. Afterward, we bid our adieu and returned to the truck. Harry raced on through Fitches Creek, pelted by more questions, through Parham village and on to a remote peninsula pointing its crooked finger at North Sound.

Running along with North Sound on the left, the road changed from broken asphalt to pure white clam shells. The glare was painful to the eyes. Harry slowed as the road roughened, drifting along to the sound of tires crunching shells---and more questions. It was late morning. The road reflected dry heat back into the cab of the pickup. The windows were open, but the metal frame was too hot to lean on. The very air seemed dead. Air conditioning? Not in an Air Force truck!

We approached the antenna farm for the high frequency receivers. In a perfectly flat, dead stubble grass field a half dozen open girder towers reached 120 feet into the air, supported by wide ranging anchor cables. Finally, *finally* Harry offered me an unsolicited comment. "We just finished painting all those towers; the salt air off the Atlantic makes corrosion control a constant effort."

Turning to him with the most seriously interested face and solemn voice I could muster, I asked, "Harry, I don't understand. When your guys get finished with the painting up there, how---how do they get down with all that wet paint?"

For a good five seconds, the only sound was the scrunching of tires. We drifted past the tower closest to the road. Harry stared straight down the road in utter disbelief, knuckles turning white across the top of the steering wheel; veins stood out on his neck! Without taking a breath, in a slow, measured voice he began, "Oh, no, Major, the painters start at the top of the mast and paint as they work their way down." He didn't--- actually--- finish--- the sentence.

The truck was sliding toward the right ditch! Harry slumped across the steering wheel face down, foot jammed on the brake. His whole torso heaved and jerked; he uttered breathless gagging sounds. "Harry, Harry! You OK?" The truck jerked to a stop at the edge of the ditch. Harry's whole body twitched and heaved. Heart attack! I reached for the radio mike. Harry's right hand shot across the bench seat, grabbing my wrist. "Don't call! Don't call!" he croaked.

He came up gasping for air, covered with tears, shaking with gales of laughter. In mid-sentence it had become perfectly clear. In mid-sentence he had realized; in mid-sentence he understood. In the midst of his anger and frustration, he had---been had! The "ignorant" Major had played him all the way down the road, in and out of tech sites and across the island for two hours.

Now, we both fought for self-control. He brought the truck back on the road and crept forward toward the receiver building. It was good that no one else was there. It would have been too embarrassing: two grown, professional men in such a state. Like preteens, we stared down the road with solemn looks, bursting into laughter if either dared a sidelong glance. Slowly, we gained control, stopping at the receiver building. As we dismounted, I confessed what he finally guessed. I was well prepared for command. I knew the answers to most of my questions.

The receiver building was a flat roofed concrete block affair, about the size of a two car garage. Unmanned and packed with automated electronics, it was surrounded by a tall chain link and barbwire security fence. The building's stark white paint reflected the dry tropic heat and glare, but the electronics inside created their own heat. To compensate, a car sized air conditioner sat on the roof. What do air conditioners produce? Cool air inside, hot air outside, and condensate --- lots of cold water. Enough to....

As the drought intensified, Harry had taken pity on the cattle in that field. He installed a long pipe from the air conditioner outflow through the fence

30

and over the lip of a pure white concrete block Air Force funded watering trough. I'll bet Air Force auditors never found *that* on the books! It gave plenty of cool water to drink, enough to splash over the side, creating a muddy oasis of fresh green grass at the edge of a large and very dead field.

Nearby, two cows lay chewing cud, ignoring their life sustaining benefactor. Gazing into those cud chewing bovine faces, we recognized our own hunger. The transmitter site further up the road would have to wait another day. Harry wheeled that pickup around and we raced to the base – no more questions. Back at main base, Harry parked in front of the chow hall and headed up the hill to check on the outcome of his early morning shop crisis. I went straight to lunch.

*

After lunch, finally at the desk, I dove into the in-basket to see what my predecessor had left for my discretion, checked the out-basket to see if he had committed me to anything on his last day or two, and read his last monthly report to Colonel Payne, our commander at Patrick AFB (the Cape Canaveral headquarters base.) Then I started to work the phone, making appointments for courtesy calls to various ministers of the Antiguan Government. Jeannie and I already had paid our respects to His Excellency, Governor Sir Wilfred and Lady Jacobs at Government House.

Came a knock on my office door, followed by the immediate entrance of the "Pahn Ahm Base" Manager and my predecessor Major S_____, who had handed over his command to me that morning. Coming through the door, the Base Manager was already speaking. "You have a problem!" he announced. I motioned to chairs, but they would have none of it. "You have a problem. The base is overrun with Antiguans after hours. It's so crowded nobody can get a seat in the club snack bar. Antiguans park their kids on base and go bar hopping all over the island past midnight. Kids are running wild all over the base, in the outdoor theater, even in the club bar. It's been going on too long and it's getting worse. *You've got to do something!*"

"I just sat down, Major S_____! You've been here for two years. Why haven't you done something?!" I enquired.

He ignored my sarcasm. "Well, you've got to do something," he said. The Base Manager nodded his head in agreement. They looked like nervous teens standing in the principal's office. Sarcasm unabated, I thanked them for their concern. They left as abruptly as they had entered.

Jeannie, our two daughters, and I had been on island at the Halcyon Cove for two weeks in preparation, spending our evenings on base; enjoying the warm tropical breezes and club amenities. We saw it all; it was exactly as described! The whole situation was a screaming security issue; rife with opportunity for theft, misuse of government funds and property, drug abuse, property damage, personal injury and loss of, or damage to the free roaming children of several nations.

Now that I was in command --- it was my problem! Still, I could not just slam the gate closed to all Antiguans. It was their island; their good will had to be sustained. I was not going to initiate my command with an all island uproar!

The base was the next best thing to a trip to the States. (We said "base" and "station" interchangeably, depending on context.) The base provided jobs for around 90 Antiguans and a place to enjoy things American without paying import duties. In an evening at the club they could enjoy cheap cocktails, the snack bar's American hamburgers and fries, hot dogs, cold drinks and ice cream at an affordable price and free movies at the open air theatre. These things were rare to non-existent in the Antiguan economy. They especially appreciated free, clean, US quality water to drink, with more to take home for their families. (With the drought, the Antiguan water system was running between nasty and empty.)

Besides, some of those after hour visitors were government officials, local businessmen and guests of our US employees. I had to maintain their good will for sure. How to proceed? It seemed time for a head clearing walk up the street.

The commander's office occupied the south end of a long, single story building on the main drag. The south wall of my office, all louvered glass windows, opened out to a bed of banana trees, close outside. The rest of the building contained offices of the Base Manager, Instrumentation Manager and our shared secretary; then the chow hall, the kitchen and finally the base laundry at the far north end. A single story barracks, the main gate road and the water works followed to the north; opposite these two buildings, east across the street, three more barracks. The carpenter, electric, plumbing, metal works, and motor pool repair shops; the power plant and fuel tanks were in a parallel line up the low hill directly to the west behind the office and barracks row. The club, open air theatre, supply Quonset sheds and motor pool parking were up the same low hill, but to the south, facing the shop row.

I only had taken a few steps outside when a real shouting match started up. Inside at the kitchen windows two Antiguan cooks were in a face off; only a fight seemed unlikely. In the midst of their loud debate they were smiling, laughing, and touching each other's shoulder in a universal gesture of friendship. In a good natured way, they were hotly discussing some minor point of appropriate Christian behavior. Theirs' was hardly a sophisticated theological discussion enriched by esoteric language, but they were earnestly serious in their friendly debate.

Continuing, I passed an elderly Antiguan gardener and stopped to chat. He seemed quite nervous at being addressed by "the Maja", but relaxed and opened up as I expressed genuine concern, inquiring about his family, working conditions and fringe benefits. "No, Maja, ah jus wuks fo de Pahn Ahm Base. Dae jus pay wen we wuk." He didn't put it this way, but Antiguan laborers with families to support generally worked hard lifelong until they dropped. He accepted that as the way things were, but also seemed deeply to consider my comments of sympathy and appreciation for his work. The base grounds really looked good despite the drought and I told him so.

An old Christian culture is found

There were many related encounters over the next several days and weeks in government offices, on the base and on the street; all consistently related enough to reveal a National character. And I remembered the humble, cheerful character of "Gumzee" the taxi driver from years earlier, who had spoken at length about his life as a working man while conducting an island tour for two young officers. Generations of poverty and servitude had created a people of great humility, acceptance, peace, joy and hope. Of course there were exceptions, but most exhibited a cheerful Faith similar to that which was resident in my Catholic wife! From my agnostic point of view, I marveled at their hope against hope, their peace and humor in sometimes difficult circumstances; recognizably, they lived simple Christian virtue and practice in the flesh.

There was much to learn about their culture.
Proceed with caution and due diligence!

Antiguan coat of arms

A summer day at St. John's open air market

II. Reins of Culture – Summer, 1977

Do not fear, O soil; be glad and rejoice…. Do not fear, you animals of the field. For the pastures of the wilderness are green! For He has given the early rain for your vindication, he has poured down for you abundant rain, the early and the later rain, as before. The threshing floors shall be full of grain and the vats shall overflow with wine and oil. You shall eat in plenty and be satisfied….
Joel 2:21-27 NRSV

Al Von Levern, Chief of Security, revealed there was a pass system for guest access; that it had been given out indiscriminately to one and all. He was delighted at my security concerns and anxious to clean up the mess. The Base Manager and Commander had ignored Von's own concerns for too long. In just a few minutes at his office near the main gate, we devised the cure.

The current "system" was terminated with a two week notice to the Government of Antigua (GOA). Each US employee was given two controlled guest passes. Records were kept. US employees could give a pass to any two Antiguan families: the hook was that the employee was held responsible for the behavior of his guests. In addition, I issued protocol passes to government and business people, but only if they had a professional function related to base requirements. With that proviso, Major S_____'s protocol list was reduced 20%. No one knew how many of the old passes had been issued to the Antiguan public, but it soon appeared the evening crowd at the club and snack bar was reduced by two thirds. The Satellite Club manager, previously suspected of hand- in- till disease, was not at all happy about that.

The base population split over the new guest policy; some predicted dire consequences (which did not happen), but others out of earshot of the Base Manager thanked me for taking control. The Governor and Eric Challenger, Secretary for External Affairs and Defense, my two primary official contacts, quietly expressed their support. However, the laid back country club attitude did not go quietly. The first incident occurred right away.

Two of our US employees ran afoul of the Navy. Yes, there was a small US Navy Facility (NAVFAC) just half a mile up the road. They had their own guest policy. Our US employees had access to the Navy exchange, commissary and club. They could even bring Antiguan guests to the Navy club, but they were required to stay together and leave together. Our gracious duo got sloshed one tropical evening and attempted to leave the NAVFAC club sans guests---twice! Each time they were admonished and sent back to round up their guests.

Their departure succeeded on the third attempt during a changing of the guard; the guests being discovered in the Navy club at midnight closing with no sponsor in sight. The NAVFAC commander called me the following morning.

We decided on a one and only warning. Next time, NAVFAC would be put off limits to anyone who blatantly defied NAVFAC policies. That was more serious than you might think. NAVFAC had the only US commissary and exchange on the island. Without access, the rare US goods found in town would have to be purchased with a stiff import tariff. The indiscretion of these two was just a hint of things to come.

*

Jeannie, meantime, was handling the home front. The Air Force had continued the lease on my predecessor's house; a two bedroom, wood frame, single wall dwelling owned by Jack Johnson. We lived in the house that Jack built! Single wall? Standard tropical practice. Lumber was imported at great expense; the year 'round average temperature was in the mid- eighties. Who needed double walls? No one had air conditioning or heat and certainly no insulation. Doors and windows had screens and fixed wooden louvered shutters, but no glass. Let the tropic winds blow through! And no locks on any of the doors and windows, except common screen latches.

The house sat near the middle of a five acre plot adjoining Jack's elderly mother's house. The elder Johnsons brought their construction company to Antigua in the early 40's to build a US bomber base, made their fortune and decided to stay. Our house had two tiny out buildings on the west side, a laundry room built on the top slab of the underground catchment basin and a guest "room" just big enough to house two cots. Oh! And a 25X45 foot swimming pool. Not leased to be sure, but available at the east side of the north facing house. The entire place needed maintenance now! Jeannie could manage the home front: our two little daughters, Dorset, the maid, and Jack Johnson's elderly gardener and maintenance crew. I had a base to run!

Until Jeannie's panic call to my office, that is. "They're painting the house an awful plum color and they won't stop. Come make them stop!" I was busy, but Jeannie was not in a negotiating mood. I was home in ten minutes to witness four Antiguan painters attacking the house with sure enough plum paint. A favorite color of Antiguans to be sure, but Jeannie had to have yellow. I approached the nearest painter, who pretended not to understand American English. I decided to practice my new found Antiguan-English dialect, but it made little difference.

"Who de baas, mon?"

"Ova dar, Maja." They knew the uniform, not me personally. Everyone at the north and west end of the island knew the "Maja" of the "Pahn Ahm Base".

"Pardon me, would you please stop painting the house? We would like you to use yellow paint."

"Ah no wuk fo you, mon."

"But could you stop while we talk about this?"

"No, mon, Ah no wuk fo you." We went through this futile exchange two or three times. He did not slow his brush strokes in the slightest, and over my shoulder, there were three others pressing ahead, making plum good time.

"Who do you wuk, uh, work for?"

"Ah wuk fo Jack Johnson, Maja. He say plum fo de haas."

Jeannie and the house continued to turn purple – plum – at a steady pace while I went to the phone. (The Antiguan phone system was up and running that week!) Of course, Jack was not in his office so I explained the matter to the secretary, who spoke English-English.

The workmen did not return the next day and all was quiet until Friday. Jack's secretary called me at the base. They searched the entire island; had found just one gallon of yellow paint. If they mixed it evenly with six gallons of white paint, they could paint the house a pale yellow. Would that do? It would. I had seen many lovely pastel yellow houses on Bermuda several years earlier. (Yes, I was on an official visit to Bermuda, not goofing off; we were building a radar site on the west end.)

The quartet was back at dawn Monday with a gallon of the ugliest baby pooh yellow that we had ever seen, but after pouring it back and forth with the white paint for half an hour, it was just right. Jack had been careful to tell his crew, "Do what the Major says. If he likes the color, if he says paint the house, then paint the house yellow."

The workman thought this very odd, to paint a house yellow. There was nothing like it anywhere else on the island. They had never seen a yellow house. However, Jeannie was happy, so I was happy. I left the quartet to their work; I had a base to run.

I returned home that evening after the workmen had gone home. Crossing the cattle guard and driving up the gentle slope, the panorama of house and out buildings really looked good, even classic; pastel yellow with white trim and no plum in sight. And there was the white picket fence at the pool. Beautiful! Pastoral! "Go look in back," Jeannie said.

During the afternoon, the trade winds picked up, blowing dust and dead leaves around. To protect the wet paint, the workmen built a temporary plywood wall eight feet high along the south and east walls of the house; the bedrooms, to be precise. The great wall of Antigua did an admirable job of protecting the paint, but as we discovered at bedtime, it also blocked the air flow through the house. We suffered a very hot night, but finally got to sleep.

To awaken in defenseless terror! We were new and alone out in the countryside of a foreign country with two little girls; hearing footsteps and muffled voices and sounds of something being dragged along the ground, just beyond the louvered shutters and that wall! We couldn't see anything, but we certainly were hearing it. We lay there helpless in quiet terror, hoping they would stay outside and leave. Finally, thankfully, they did. When we were sure, we slept.

In the morning, I walked around back to investigate. The next thing Jeannie heard beyond the great wall was laughter. In the bare, dusty soil alongside the wall, hoof prints! Cows! And long grooves and scratches left by the chains they dragged. Muffled voices? Cow snorts and moans scrambled by the trade winds and muffled by the walls and louvered shutters.

Cow chains? Antiguan law required cows to be fenced or chained. However, the law did not specify that the chain be connected to anything, so farmers provided the required chain and allowed cattle to roam free about the island in search of water and grass, dragging a chain wherever they went.

While discussing bovine contributions to Antiguan culture, it would be impolite not to recognize the cultural role of geckos, cats, dogs, horse spiders and burros. Within the house, across the ceiling and halfway down the wall, half a dozen geckos ruled. They were most appreciated, as efficient as any commercial pest exterminator. Mr. Fluff, the long haired black cat who welcomed us to his home upon our arrival, played the same role up to his maximum jumping height and throughout his range of personal interest.

The Gecko, Terror of the House Fly

The front porch, old brick on a concrete slab, was neutral territory. The dogs respected Mr. Fluff's right to lounge there in the shade by the front door, but ruled in the yard away from the immediate house. They, the dogs, wandered freely about the island. Upon finding an unguarded house, they would set up a perimeter, loudly announce their intent to be employed, and if payment in food and water was forthcoming in a reasonable time, would thereafter guard the house from evildoers. We fondly remember Babee, named by our maid Dorset Lincoln, Patches named after his calico coat, and Robert E. Lee, so named because a friendly American couple from the base had named their dog General Grant.

Horse spiders? Hairy brown bodies as big as your hand, eight hairy brown legs as long as your fingers, pincers that could send you to Holburton Hospital and they could clear a one meter high jump. Fortunately, they respected Mr. Fluff and were rarely seen close to the house. Their only problem was a fatal, drought driven attraction to the swimming pool. They could get in for a drink, but could not exit.

Horse spider, terror of the yard pest

Cows, you may know, will not cross a cattle guard for fear of breaking a leg between the pipes. They entered the yard that one time through a broken fence somewhere in back of the house.

Burros on the other hand, are resourceful, often brazen critters. I was returning from a jog over past Cedar Grove and on to Blue Waters Hotel; stopped near, but not under, a Manchaneel tree (a vicious bit of creation that dipped its roots in the Atlantic's salt water at roadside and dripped poison from its leaves.) I had a clear view of our driveway.

Why I never stopped under that tree while jogging.

Papa, Momma, and baby burro were in the road, surveying our cattle guard. Papa burro demonstrated the crossing technique: he lay down close to the cattle guard, rolled across on his back and ambled up our driveway! In like manner, mamma and baby burro.

One evening, I was just up the road half a mile to the east enjoying the cocktail party de jour. Jeannie stayed home with the kids that night, not feeling so well. Shortly after ten, she called me in a panic. You guessed it. (Through the closed, louvered shutters,) "I can hear several people walking out there on the front porch, whispering quietly!" In great jogging condition, I sprinted home. Leaping the cattle guard and rounding a nearby flamboyant tree, I got a clear picture of the house in the moonlight --- and a clear picture of Papa burro, Mamma burro and baby burro *on the front porch!*

Burro at lunch in the front yard

41

Weeks later, Colonel Payne, my boss, and Major General Marshall, his boss, spent the night in our little two cot guest house, awaiting a C-141 flight to Ascension. They came up to the house for an early breakfast, trembling from a strange mixture of shock and laughter. Over their first cup of coffee, (and the overhead roar of their inbound C-141 ride to Ascension), they explained.

Guest house guarded by Mr. Lee

It had been a hot night. They left the shutters open between and at the head of the two cots. At the first crack of dawn, Papa burro stuck his head in the window between the cots and gave them his best and loudest alarm clock braaaay; not more than two feet from each sleeping head! He was far more effective, far louder than a flock of roosters!

But more often, the dogs and the burros treated us to their Ode to Joy, taking turns chasing each other back and forth at a relaxed canter around the back yard tamarind tree. All this was to the tune of joyous, playful barking and braying.

*

In the midst of this Pastoral Paradise of Joy, this tropic Garden of Eden, Harry found an opportunity for friendly revenge. In the first weeks as I met, stopped and chatted with most base personnel, Antiguans and Americans alike; I made a lot of good natured noise about the Maja's brand new, shiny black, *almost regulation* Air Force boots. It seemed a great way to break the ice on the way to convincing the contractor personnel that I was not there to police them, but to assist them any way I could. I wore those boots around the base spit and polished. They were beautiful, but the rough shod, more that tropically casual civilian personnel were not impressed.

Harry came into my office one hot tropical summer morning with a worried look about him. "Major, we have a problem; you need to see." I was busy, but he insisted. "Major, you must see this!" We hopped into his pickup truck, swung left out the main gate and drove around to a dirt access road running along the back chain link fence. We got out of the truck next to a large, dense field of Cassie growing on a gentle slope that led down toward the Atlantic. Three or four of his work crew were waiting in a small clearing.

Acacia tortuosa

Cassie bushes resemble six or eight foot high tumble weeds before they break loose and start a-tumbling. Cassie grows wild in the north and east of the island, thick and thorny, making for an unpleasant traverse on foot, especially in tropical summer heat amidst swarms of flies. Harry led his crew single file into the thicket, straight away from the fence, pushing deeper into the Cassie for a hundred feet or so, with me at the rear. The dry heat was intense. Vaguely, I noticed Harry, then each of his crew in line, took an extra long step *at the same place.* Concentrating on Cassie avoidance, I did not respond. Too late, I noticed the disturbed ground over *that same place*, that the flies were extra thick at *that same place*, and the smell. My beautiful, *almost regulation* Air Force boots sank ankle deep into the muck.

43

Harry and his crew turned back with broad smiles. "That's what I wanted to show you, Major." Harry announced. "The sewer line from Coolidge village up there has broken where it crosses our easement to the radar site. Our underground power lines and communication circuits are at risk."

"Not to mention my boots," I offered. With a good laugh, we all agreed it was a real problem, the sewage, not my boots; more specifically, my problem since it involved the fledgling Antiguan Government. Forget the boots. The sewage problem fell right into my lap. We headed back to the office and I called the Antigua Public Utility Authority (APUA.).

That is when the Carnival began. I mean that with double entendre. In Antigua, nothing gets done by the APUA or anybody else during carnival season, unless it has directly to do with parade floats, steel band competitions, or queen pageants. Sewage poured out on our cables and oozing down to the Atlantic did not make the list. But we, that is to say "de Pahn Ahm Base", was on their list.

Throughout the latter half of July we were inundated with requests for party ice (rare on the Antiguan economy), party trays (not just trays to be sure, but loaded with flocks of US fried chicken or sandwiches), "loan" of tarps never seen again, conduct of base briefings and tours for teen and adult queen contestants. We even hosted a cocktail party at the Satellite Club honoring Caribbean queens from eleven other colonies, states and nations. I was personally involved with every bit, except the last. Range scheduling at Cape Canaveral was unkind enough to schedule a missile launch during the party. I had to be at the range safety console in the secure, windowless communications center, just in case I had to blow the thing up!

We provided and decorated the Carnival Queen's float (read our flatbed semi-truck and trailer). I even participated in uniform at the opening ceremony of carnival on the Saint John's cricket field (cricket *pitch*, in English-English) right on the official Government of Antigua reviewing stand next to the very surprised Governor of Antigua. (They had not invited me, but with Sir Wilfred's nervous assent, I stood at his right shoulder. He had no idea what I was doing there.)

Carnival Queen

During the march by of the Royal Antigua Police Force marching band and the Defense Force Cadre, I saluted the Antiguan flag in full view of the assembled multitude. It probably wasn't protocol to do so from the British or US point of view. However, there was a quiet, emotional transition toward independence going on and I had the authority to represent the US government. The recognition and respect I showed the Antiguan flag must have resulted in a strong emotional response. Though not fully comprehending the impact of my actions at the time, I do know that after that day, my working relationship with the Government of Antigua was tight, close and mutually supportive right to the top. A little show of humility and respect goes a long way!

Finally, I attended the Eastern Caribbean steel band competition in a quasi-official capacity, all for the sake of public relations, of course. What a hardship tour! Oh! I almost forgot.

During that same two weeks our crew, crane and clamshell bucket worked for nine days to dig out and clear the sump and outlet for Potworks dam. Potworks reservoir, formerly a large lake, was cracked mud dry except for one pitiful, caked over and hidden mud puddle about 20 feet from the dam outlet (pardon my French) which, of course, I found the hard way with my beautiful *almost regulation* Air Force boots; but the end of the drought was predicted. August brought quick relief in two ways.

*

Most importantly to the Antiguans, a gentle drought ending rain began the first night of August; converting the dry, dusty island to instant mud. Carnival revelers got wet and muddy, steel drums got a bit rusty toward the end, but nobody complained. The rain continued for two and a half months with only occasional letup, clear into early October. Our drought depleted two and a half million gallon underground water catchment (fed by water running off the WW II portion of the runway) overflowed after a week or so. Our offer to pump to the Antiguan water system was politely refused (they were full?) until someone at their water works discovered wrong valves had been turned and their supposedly quite full tanks were indeed quite empty. Problem solved, we began pumping millions of gallons into their system. Potworks reservoir filled to the brim. And the rains kept a-coming!

Most importantly to "Pahn Ahm Base", the joyful madness of carnival ended. Now everyone would get back to work. APUA would fix the sewer line; our expensive, mission critical underground cables would be secure. So I thought!

After repeated phone calls and reminders, an APUA crew showed up at the sewage leak: without equipment, not even a shovel. This happened twice, a week apart; then APUA called and washed their hands of the sewage. They said Antigua Public Health was responsible.

Public Health, of course, had no construction equipment at all to forget to bring to the job. After a month of my constant nagging and a desperate appeal to Eric Challenger, my primary government contact, late in September APUA took back responsibility. And Harry, sloshing back into the Cassie one fine day between rain showers, discovered that someone installed just enough sewer pipe to clear our easement. From there, an open stream of sewage continued its merry way toward the Atlantic.

The issue behind the issue seems to have been bureaucratic, i.e., who really was responsible (probably ill equipped Public Health?) This was my clue that the new, fledgling Government of Antigua still was sorting out roles and missions among various ministries and agencies.

As the monsoonal rains continued, we suffered a double fault on our overhead power lines to Parham Bay. Of course, we had no cherry picker. It had been swapped with Ascension for the bulldozer which now inhabited the back lot of our motor pool. In desperation, I called APUA.

Surprise! An hour later there was a fully equipped cherry picker and a most professional APUA crew working side by side with our pole climbers. The upshot was a close, long lasting mutual cooperation that resolved a number of emergencies, ours and theirs, throughout my tenure. APUA proved to be a most professional outfit.

The Antiguan fire department less so. Von prepared and conducted aircraft fire training for them on the air field. The Antiguans showed up at the hot fire drill ready for action, wearing their brand new British donated fire fighting suits; except that every one of them wore street shoes. I notified my command and Military Airlift Command at Charleston AFB that aircrews would be on their own in a hot fire crash at Antigua.

The Royal Antigua Police Force also had issues. Flight operations at Patrick AFB called to alert me that three separate C-5A sorties carrying over size radar antennas to Ascension would refuel at Antigua, one aircraft each, over the next three weeks. The C-5, one of the two largest aircraft in the world, is much larger than a Boeing 747 and much, much, much larger than our C-141s routinely seen at Antigua each week. The C-5 can carry four Greyhound busses downstairs and 250 troops with their equipment upstairs. I notified Eric downtown and made separate calls to Dennis Nanton, Airdrome Superintendent, and to the commander of the Antigua Police Force.

No Antiguan native had ever seen a C-5. I emphasized the size of the C-5A and requested security assistance. I had in mind a few police for crowd control.

On the morning of the first sortie, I discovered that the Antiguans were responding beyond my wildest expectations. They shut down the government, closed all schools and bused school children from all over the island. All of official and business and much of private Antigua was expected. Dennis closed the Airdrome to all other air traffic an hour ahead of the C-5A arrival and the Police Commander turned out the *entire* police force. It produced a huge crowd! An audience that big called for a show!

By telephone, I caught up with the pilot at breakfast in the Patrick flight line cafeteria; explained the situation. "I don't know what you can do with a loaded C-5A, but could you put on a show for the assembled multitude?" He could. *Did he!*

At the appointed hour, with the multitude scanning the skies, we first heard that other worldly low pitched characteristic C-5A moan generated by four monstrous fan jet engines. He came in on final from the Northeast. Left to right as we stood outside the terminal, he flew a fighter sweep at 350 knots (400 mph), the entire length of the main runway at 75 feet, pulled up fighter style (more like a broaching whale) and disappeared in the distance. Out of sight, he circled the entire island and approached again from the Northeast. This time, he came in just above stall speed; flaps down, wheels down with those huge fans at full power, again flying the full length of the runway at 75 feet. He flew so slowly, the C-5 seemed to hover like a monster whale drifting over the ocean bottom. Again, he circled the island and landed on the third pass.

Barely fitting his wheels to the narrow taxiways, wings reaching far beyond the edge, he gingerly taxied, agonizingly, slowly across the field, finally swinging around with a final blast from his number one engine, to park facing the side of the terminal. After a procedural minute or two those four big fan engines quieted, moaning down to all stop. Up close, the aircraft was truly enormous, blimp like, far larger than a monster, beached whale.

The Royal Antigua Police Force – all of them – cordoned off the aircraft, forming up man to man at parade rest, ten feet apart; a perfect circle entirely around the C-5. For several agonizing minutes, the entire crowd was breathlessly quiet in total awe of the sheer size of the thing. The whole Airdrome was church-quiet. All was still. No one moved. No one spoke, not a whisper.

And then, the huge clamshell cargo door encompassing the entire front of the aircraft began to open vertically, whale like; yes, like an enormous maw. Oh sweet, simple innocence of Paradise!

The Royal Antigua Police Force, to the last man, took one look at that yawning maw, broke ranks and ran away!

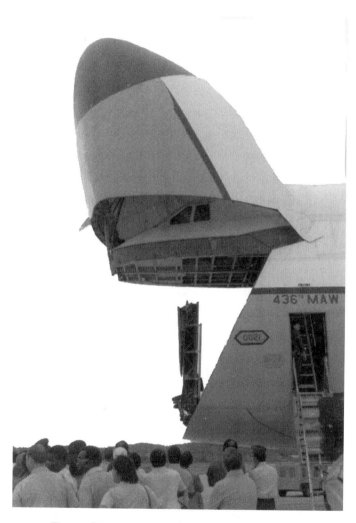

Does this picture really need a caption?

Paradise Commander leads the air crew parade

Ian Thow enters the belly of the whale

Paradise lost

III. Reign of Sin - Summer 1977

Happy, indeed is the man who follows not the counsel of the wicked; not so are the wicked, not so! They like winnowed chaff shall be driven away by the wind. Psalm 1 NRSV

During those first two months, July and August 1977, along with the cultural adjustments alluded to, our first summer in the island also was a time for house cleaning --- at the base, I mean. Jeannie, Dorset Lincoln (our maid fast becoming a friend,) the geckos and Mr. Fluff quickly established tranquility of order within our domestic paradise; while the dogs set up their surveillance of order in the yard. Everyone understood their place and role in the established order. The horse spiders (usually) stayed in the outer perimeter or at the pool fending off smaller varmints, cows respected the cattle guards, and the burros provided entertainment. Even the Antiguan fishermen played a role. They quickly found our kitchen door and provided a frequent supply of Caribbean lobsters at a pittance. The lobsters played their part as well, providing entertainment for a very cautious Mr. Fluff as they crawled around on the kitchen floor. (Dipped in New Zealand butter, they also were delicious!) Peace in Paradise. Peace in our time!

Not quite so in my professional purview; not quite so. That first minor incident with the sloshed duo over at NAVFAC, already mentioned, was a mere hint of that which was to come.

USNS Hoyt Vandenberg under way

The USNS Vandenberg, painted all pure white, was a very large range ship. It carried two large radar systems (similar to the one behind the LIAT hanger) and, amid ship, a bigger telemetry dish with all the associated electronics. It docked in St Johns at oh dark thirty one morning. (I had been rolled out of the sack after midnight, called back to the base to consult with the skipper by VHF radio and arrange for dock space. Seems he could not raise the sleeping night shift at the port on any established frequency.) Then shortly after the crew disembarked, a crew member was charged with assaulting a port guard. That started up my morning just fine!

After a blizzard of phone calls to Eric Challenger, my Government of Antigua contact; Ian Thow, my British contact, Jack Oakes and Ginny Bailey at Down Range Affairs (Patrick AFB, Florida); Military Sea Transport Service at Port Canaveral and their command at Norfolk; and finally the ambassador at Barbados; a consensus was reached: the fledgling Associated State of Antigua and Barbuda did indeed have jurisdiction. They handled the whole situation with aplomb. At a hurried inquiry the same day (the ship would sail at sunset) the case against our sailor collapsed and was thrown out. No two of a handful of witnesses could agree on what had happened down there on the docks. Every event in Paradise should be handled so easily!

It did not go down so easy with Mr. K_____, an American employee of Pan Am. Over at NAVFAC, he had purchased a freezer (OK, perhaps even commendable, he had access to the Navy exchange), but a sharp young Navy logistician noticed that the freezer was delivered to a next door neighbor, a relative of K_____'s Antiguan wife (not at all OK!) After an enquiry by Navy staff, K_____ was found to have been reimbursed by said neighbor who was totally not authorized to purchase duty free. After a short pow wow between the two commanders, we pulled K_____'s exchange privilege.

He offered a defense. We demurred. Finally, he offered me advice that we should not tell the Government of Antigua. "It would just open up a whole bunch of issues," he said. I thanked him for his advice; then reported the unauthorized sale and his advice to Eric, downtown, and to the new NAVFAC commander, Lt. Commander Dick Grant, who had just checked in. It turned out that the advice was very good, very good indeed. It did "open up a whole bunch of issues."

Abuse of NAVFAC commissary and exchange privileges was rampant! Dick began laying waste to Navy perpetrators, while the Government of Antigua was delighted to enforce bills of tariff on many of its fine citizens. The government desperately needed the money!

It was about this time the Pahn Ahm Base Manager announced he was transferring to another base. His departure was sudden and unlamented. He was replaced by one Jim Edwards. Apparently, Pan Am executives knew there was a problem they had to fix.

A few days later, I was on a telecom with senior Air Force staff at Patrick AFB when the subject came up. I was told, "Yes, Jim is Pan Am's hatchet man. When there is trouble at a base, that's who they send. You can depend on him."

Hatchet man? I had never thought of myself that way, but it fit my role, too; and Dick over at NAVFAC was swinging his own hatchet, with all the exchange and now drug abuse he was uncovering. We had a troika of hatchets in play, apparently long overdue! (The drug investigation started when a young sailor, while talking to the XO, dropped his pen.

When he bent over to pick it up, a package of marijuana fell out of his uniform shirt pocket.)

Also, according to Pan Am auditors, the Satellite Club manager on my base was suspected of "poor management and excessive losses." (Read suspicion of hand-in-till disease and drinking the profits with the assistance of friends.) The auditors threatened to padlock the club. The manager hung on 'till August, when he found it prudent to resign. Over my objections, he was replaced with Mr. T_____. He was burdened with the same suspicions, but no one else would take the job. (A year or so later he and his wife fled the island, never to be seen again, when Von and I walked up the hill and padlocked the club at dawn. Pan Am auditors were inbound on the afternoon C-141 flight. It did not take them long to find evidence of fraud and embezzlement.)

In the midst of the club mess, the Eastern Test Range base inspector flew in from Patrick AFB. I was more than a little peeved. I did not want to be blamed for the mess I inherited, but the inspector seemed to know what was going on before he arrived. He gave us a "Satisfactory" rating; room to get credit for improvements and if not, room for blame. Fair enough!

Soon reports began to circulate around the base that "The Major" was showing up at random times day and night: in the communications center at two in the morning, driving through the shops area at 10pm, at the chow hall coffee pot at four am, wandering through the offices, the club, talking to people he met. It is amazing what you learn speaking with the least Antiguan or US worker. Equally amazing how folks shaped up, realizing I could pop up at any moment, day or night. But never as a "gotcha", always as "Jim (or Harry), you might want to check on ….

*

It had been trying all the way across the chow hall, sliding from side to side, rocking back and forth on the tray. Finally, as I placed the tray on the table opposite Harry, the tall, narrow bottle of hot sauce executed a classic tree fall across my plate of much too wet grits. Harry ignored the splatter that descended upon his hands and sleeves; he was concentrating on his usual morning starter plate of scrambled eggs, hash browns and bacon. You had to take it on faith that there were eggs under there. All you could see was a thick carpet of black pepper. Every morning he shook the black stuff on until *all* the yellow disappeared. "Like pepper, huh? Is that a Brazilian thing or a Harry thing?" I inquired.

"Problem!" he mumbled through a mouthful of hash browns.

"Think I'll go sit with Jim," I offered.

Harry wiped his face and continued, "No joke, Major. We've been losing building supplies for a few months. Thought it was just paperwork, but everything signed out was used and everything used was signed out. And it's not stuff stashed at work sites. Yesterday, Von saw some gutter pipes and straps out in the cassie behind the supply Quonset. There is more there this morning. It looks like someone is throwing things over the fence to pick up later."

"Any idea who?"

"J_____ is building himself a retirement home over at Sweets; been with us a long time. He's my most senior Antiguan, my best foreman. I hope he's not the one, but we'll see. Von can't trust Antiguan security on this one, so he is going to stay on base and watch. Keep you posted." Harry headed for the dish dump. I took the remains of my eggs and grits and that bottle of hot sauce over to Jim's table.

I stayed home for breakfast next morning; didn't see Harry 'till lunch at that same table on the back wall of the chow hall. We were well away from the dish dump, the serving line and prying ears. "Got 'em," Harry announced. "Von has Polaroids of him loading up his pickup. He waited a few minutes, then drove over to J_____'s new house. Got pictures of him unloading our stuff at the house. Nice house!"

Harry continued. "We tried to fire him this morning, but J_____ refuses to leave and F_____ says the union will strike. J_____ needs his pay check to finish the house, now that we've cut his supply line. Nobody in town will pay him near what he makes out here as senior foreman. F_____ admits the obvious, but likes being the union rep; he won't confront the rank and file. He's been a fair, evenhanded union steward; so we need to protect his job." Suddenly, the ball was back in my court. Union problems quickly became government problems down town.

Under the Status of Forces Agreement I had no "de jure" jurisdiction over civilian crimes, but I had a great deal of "de facto" going for us. And, there was the power of "the favor." In a poor economy, barter makes things work. The medium of exchange was the barter of goods or services, the usual place of negotiation, the cocktail party or on occasion, the annual Royal Antigua Police Force dining-in. It just required a little finesse, knowledge of the socio-politico-economic environment and especially, stealth. Since we were constantly granting favors to various ministries of the Government of Antigua, they were delighted to return a favor.

A call to the commander of the Royal Antigua Police Force made the matter clear. We had incontrovertible evidence of a crime. Loss of a coveted job should be sufficient punishment. If J_____ resigned, we would not press charges. But there was this little problem that the union was protecting him, obviating his departure. Could CID (Central Investigative Division) explain the matter to Mr. J_____?

They could. Since the union was associated with the opposition party, the requested favor would stick it to the opposition publicly and promote trouble in their ranks. Surely that was a good thing. The commander expressed appreciation for our previous assistance and our mutual quasi-military association. He assured us of his assistance.

That same afternoon, two CID plainclothesmen presented themselves at the gate. We offered them the privacy of a room in an empty barracks across the street from my office and the chow hall, introducing them to a very nervous Mr. J_____. We left so they could discuss the matter of purloined construction material in private.

Their discussion lasted less than ten minutes. From the offices across the street we watched CID depart. Right behind them, J_____ rushed across the street and up the hill to Harry's office asking if he (oh please!), if it might be permissible that he resign. Please!

Harry suggested that he need not present the customary two week notice; collected his base pass.

Harry was losing a good friend under tragic circumstances. J_____ was just a few weeks away from Pan Am retirement, a rare fringe benefit in Antigua. He lost everything.

What did CID say to him? Some things you just don't want to know!

*

B_____'s story was tragic in a different way. It began when Von dropped by my office. "I was doing my monthly fire inspection in A Barracks. I found this!" He had two roaches in an evidence bag --- not that kind, the half smoked marijuana joint kind. They were in an ash tray in B_____'s room, both warm, one still smoking. The smell we knew so well was evident (We both had had the training.) The evidence made the trip to Patrick where it was positively ID'd.

Not only was marijuana illegal, but drug intoxication easily could impact the mission. As the saying goes, if I told you what B_____ 's job was at the radar site, I would have to shoot you! He had to go. That decision caused an uproar! The managers descended on my office to appeal.

"You can't do this to us. We need him at the radar site. He has the training, the skills, compartmented Top Secret security clearances desperately needed at the radar site. Those clearances are almost impossible for civilians to obtain. He's been on base less than a month and besides, the brand new van he shipped to the island has just arrived. Major, have mercy!"

Clearances needed are clearances obtainable. The van comment suggested that convenience and contract compliance was as much an issue to them as the delay in obtaining clearances and skills.

Knowing full well that if I yielded, I would continue to have drug problems the rest of my tenure, I gave them an easy choice. There was a C-141 on the ramp that same afternoon, loading retro-grade cargo and passengers for the States. Manifest him on that flight back to Patrick AFB, or.... If he was still on the island when the plane took off, I would give full particulars, Von's testimony and the evidence report to CID.

Oh, by the way, the Antiguan jail was stone built as a small British fort in the early18th century. As far as we knew, it had not been refurbished or upgraded. Not a nice place for a young white boy to spend the night entertaining the lesser lights of black Antigua. His van? It could remain on base until shipped back to the States. It was not to be sold in Antigua.

I assure you, he was on the airplane. He slept safely, if not peaceably that night, in Florida.

There were no winners. We needed his skills. The Air Force pulled his clearances and after a week or so of careful deliberation and the doting and crossing of legalistic i's and t's back at Patrick AFB, RCA fired him. Never again would he be able to work in government or in any civilian job needing a security clearance; a very bright, perhaps brilliant and capable young man caught up in youthful foolishness.

Rolling Terror: the Vehicle of Mercy and Justice

IV. Reign of Mercy and Justice
September 1977

These are the sacrifices most pleasing to God: mercy, humility, praise, peace, charity. Such as these, then, let us bring and, free from fear, we shall await the coming of the Judge who will judge the world in equity... the peoples in his truth.

Saint Augustine, Bishop

Mid-morning, I was at my desk writing the August monthly report for the staff at Patrick AFB. The internal base phone on my desk rang out an urgent alarm. It was Von. "Benny just came through the gate. He stopped to ask the guard where you were; then blew through the gate without permission. He's looking for *you*, Major!"

"Fine," I said, "if you see him again, give him directions. So who is Benny?"

"Didn't I tell you? He is the bouncer at the casino. He is the Island enforcer!"

"Oh, *that* Benny." I was cool, military-professional. "Thanks, Von."

Back to the monthly report, but I noticed the background noise from across the hall in the offices of the Base Manager, Instrumentation Manager and our shared secretary diminished into crypt like silence. Clearly, Von had alerted them to impending doom.

Outer door opened. Outer door closed. Heavy footsteps. Muffled deep voice at the secretary's desk. More utter silence except for heavy foot falls in the hall. Forceful knock on office door. No other sounds, *anywhere*! The whole base seemed to hunker down, to know who or what was at my door. "Yes?" I responded in my best military-professional voice.

An almost crisp British accent echoed in the hall. "May ah speak with you, Sah!?"

"Of course, please come in."

Benny entered my office in a stoop, squeezing sideways through the door frame. Used to gauging ceiling height, he stood up carefully under the seven foot ceiling, head between the light fixtures. He was that big! He was black, of African descent, three times my small boned 135 pounds and wore an exquisitely tailored three piece, pinstripe navy blue suit and tie. Stunning!

I tried to look pleasant, non-threatening!

Dodging more light fixtures, he crossed the room, leaned over my desk and placed his ham-fisted (accurate, not a trite expression); he placed his hands on the opposite corners of my executive size desk. He spoke again.

"Sah! Mah name is Benny. Ah wuks at the casino. Ahm a patient man, Sah (!), but if I don't get satisfaction soon (!), ahm going to have to start breaking wrists, Sah!"

It seemed inopportune to inquire of whose wrists he had in mind. I slowly slid mine, still firmly attached to my hands and arms, onto my lap, under the desk. "Oh, I don't think you need to do that, Benny. Please sit down and tell me, what is the problem?" I wasn't sure what would crack first, me or the chair toward which I motioned, but he did sit down. So far, the chair and I were doing well. Benny warmed up to his story.

Benny owned the only Cadillac in all Antigua (Painted all white like the USNS Vandenberg, only not quite so large!) To be sure, on a small island just nine by eighteen miles large, every one of the 70,000 residents knew whose Cadillac it was. They also were aware of his work related talents; so the sight of an oncoming, most imposing white Cadillac elicited instant respect island wide, if not outright flight. It was this Cadillac and none other that M_____ and her boyfriend had sideswiped on a very dark midnight ride, two weeks earlier. The hapless pair were radar technicians at the base. M_____, blind drunk, was driving. The boyfriend was passed out on the back seat. He slept through M_____'s near death experience.

Benny, who had responded like any upright, concerned citizen, spent the next two weeks trying to get now-very-sober-and-terrified M_____ to pay up for repairs, without success. Our two employees had responded in a most un-American way by holing up at the military secure radar site, sleeping on the floor behind the operations console, and receiving food packages and (probably) bottles of cheer from sympathetic co-workers. The radar site was one of the few places on island secure from my new found Antiguan acquaintance.

It now appeared that M_____'s were the wrists at risk. I returned mine to the top of the desk. Clearly, my good friends the Base Manager, the Instrumentation Manager and Von, had kept me in the dark for two weeks. "I'm sorry, this is the first I have heard about your accident. There must be a solution to your problem. Give me a week or so to investigate. I'll give you a call."

He stood, (looking for the light fixtures) allowed me the week; reminded me of the wrist risk. In response, I totally surprised both of us: I inquired about his family and island of birth. He utterly relaxed, sat back down, and we had the most intriguing, friendly half hour conversation. He told me of his childhood as a (small?!) boy on the island of Monserrat, how work was impossible to obtain there, and how only at the casino had he found employment in his specialized line of work. He was quite grateful to them for the opportunity to rise above island poverty. We shared both our stories in general terms, as would prudent men, and we parted on most amicable terms.

Truth was, until my question about family, he was as apprehensive about me as I was about him! He was on unfamiliar ground, a US air base, and knew it! For all he knew, I had a weapon at hand.

I did not feel so amicable. I had been hung out to dry. I reached for the phone, but sat back. Von and his two seniors were coming through the door, quite pale; expecting to find me quietly torture strangled. "What the hell are you guys doing?!" I inquired. "You *knew* that was coming!" Ignoring the question, Jim went straight to their story.

M_____ and her boyfriend, middle aged alcoholic techs, were having a normal evening down town, drinking themselves into oblivion. Around eleven, remembrance of the midnight shift surfaced in her fog bank mind. With help, the boyfriend was poured into the back seat of her pending wreck where he promptly passed out. She then set out toward the radar site at speed, over the dark-really dark- moonless and streetlight-less island terrain. That is how she met, i.e., sideswiped Benny in the dark of a merging country intersection. The problem was, M_____ and her male company were penniless; every payday, their checks converted to alcohol. She had managed to buy Antiguan car insurance, but the agent was stiffing her.

Suddenly, I was amicable, again. I gently gave them a little advice on the sharing of information; informed them as to the location of my office door. M_____'s radar supervisor consulted with her during the night shift and returned the next morning with the required agent's name and phone number.

Once alone in my office, I picked up the phone. "Good morning Benny. This is the Major. I think I have a solution for the repair of your car."

"Sah?!"

"First of all, you could break every bone in M_____'s body, and the boyfriend's, too; but that would not get you two dimes to rub together. They truly are absolutely broke. They have drunk every dime they had. But here is my idea. M_____ *does* have Antiguan car insurance. The problem is, her agent refuses her claim. He won't even listen to her. He has been less than helpful. Do you know Mr. A_____? Do you think he would listen to you?

For a few moments the only sounds were the familiar pops, hisses and squeaks of the Antiguan phone system. Then a quiet staccato "huh, huh, huh" crescendo-d into outright laughter. "Sah?! Oh, yes, Sah! Ah know just the man. Yes, Sah! Ah knows him! Oooh yes, Sah! Ah know just what to say! Yes, Sah! I know *just* what to say!"

"He should be able to help, Benny, but if he can't help, let me know. We'll try to work it out."

"Oh no, Sah. No, Sah(!) He surely will help. Ahm sure he can help, Sah(!) Yes, Sah! I know *just* what to say." More chuckles, pops, hiss, squeaks, click.

I never heard another word from anyone on the subject. No one asked questions or expressed concern. Yes, Sah! They knew just what *not* to say!

Weeks later, on my way downtown to some government meeting, I passed the very intersection where Benny and M_____ had met. There, waiting for me to pass, was the only Cadillac in all Antigua. It was beautiful: white as snow, waxed, polished, not a scratch on it, glinting in the tropical sun. But even brighter was the ear to ear grin I saw through the windshield. And there was that huge, wrist snapping hand giving a semaphore wave of happy greetings!

I responded in kind; continued to town with a grin of my own. Mercy and Justice were served.

V. 'Er Majesty's Reign - October, 1977

Her Most Excellent Majesty Elizabeth the Second, Elizabeth Alexandra Mary of Winsor, by the Grace of God, Queen of the Associated State of Antigua and Her other Realms and Territories, Head of the Commonwealth, Defender of the Faith, arrived in Antigua, WI on 28 October 1977 aboard Her Majesty's Yacht Britannia. His Royal Highness Prince Phillip Duke of Edinburgh accompanied Her Majesty. The Commander and Mrs. Hughes were privileged to ....

Monthly Activity Report, October 1977

T he Queen is coming! The Queen is coming! It was a magical, memorable time, but there are some things you just don't put in an official USAF report. Nor did it begin for us in any way that could be described as magical, though it certainly *was* memorable. It began in mid-September with a bulldozer, a forty-something bulldozer jockey and 30 acres of cassie.

Antiguans at every level of government and populace flooded us with requests for help. Everyone wanted to spruce up, put on the very best appearance for 'Er Majesty. A National race was on to whitewash everything that stood still: every government building, every private establishment, every tree and roadside rock; to mow and clear and repair and clean and paint and decorate *anything* and everything that otherwise might seem unseemly to 'Er Most Excellent Majesty's royal blue eyes. All kinds of reasonable and hair-brained assistance schemes were proposed by the daily parade of Antiguan officials, businessmen and influential citizens that called or visited my office. Under the protective umbrella of policy, I referred them all to Eric: GOA Secretary, External Affairs and Defense, for his review.

Eric was implacable in these matters; he only proposed the most critical requests for our assistance. When he took the trouble to drive out to the base, appearing unannounced at my door, I knew the GOA had a grave matter for my consideration. Until I heard his request, that is.

We were swamped with base projects funded at the end of the fiscal year. If we could not complete the projects in a timely manner, the money would be given to another base that *could* get their projects accomplished. Our most critical project required the services of the aforementioned bulldozer obtained from Ascension AFB; yet Eric was asking us to take time out to bulldoze and clear 30 acres of cassie in front of the air terminal. Seeing my back was up, Eric pulled his trump card. "I know this doesn't sound very important, Al, but the Premier personally asked me to get this done. Please, can you do it?" I really had no choice after that arm twister. I authorized assistance over the dead and quivering bodies of Jim Edwards and Harry James. *They* were angry; but Dale, an emotional Irishman, was *furious.*

Dale picked up on Harry and Jim's complaints and stoked that brush clearing task into a towering inferno of indignation, as I found out the hard way out in the field by checking on his progress. He was not impressed with my thoughtfulness. NEVER, NEVER, NEVER stand down an Irishman when his hand is on the throttle of a bulldozer! Right lever back, left lever forward; he spun the bulldozer around in its own length and headed full throttle at my staff truck. Fortunately, full throttle on a dozer is still pretty slow going. Remembering a suddenly urgent office task, I beat him to the truck and got out of there.

Over the next two weeks, Dale logged 118 hours on the dozer clock, all dedicated to 'Er Majesty. In the meantime, we got mail. It was hand delivered from the Governor's office: a 6"x 9" cream colored envelope with the Queen's Royal Crest printed in red on the flap. Sliding the very heavy cream colored, gold embossed card from the envelope, we read:

EIIR

The Master of the Household
is commanded by Her Majesty to invite

Major Albert E. Hughes USAF & Mrs Hughes .

to a Reception to be given by
The Queen and The Duke of Edinburgh
on board H.M. Yacht "Britannia" at St. John's
on Friday, 28th October, 1977, at 9.45 p.m.

A reply is requested to:
Private Secretary to the Governor,
Governor's Residence,
Antigua,
Tel: 20003
Guests are asked to arrive between 9.25 and 9.45 p.m.

Dress: Dinner Jacket
Lounge Suit
Decorations

We were going to be presented to the Queen! Eric told me there was stiff competition in the government for the limited invites. Consensus was, only British subjects would be invited, but Governor, Sir Wilfred stepped in personally, ordering four invitations to be set aside for the two base commanders and their wives. News of this courtesy spread rapidly across NAVFAC and the air base."

Dale was at my office door quick as a wind driven cassie fire, but my first impulse was to send him to the showers. He was an unshaven mess; clothed in greasy, threadbare shorts, oversized holy tennis shoes (no socks), and a burr covered, sweat and grease stained, sleeveless and torn tee shirt. He had just come in from a day of dozing in the tropic sun. Bulldozing, I mean.

"You need a chauffeur!" he announced. I didn't think so. "Everybody on the island will be in Saint John's. There'll be traffic jams everywhere you need to go. You need to relax and enjoy the day!" I declined. Dale dropped his own trump card. "Besides, you owe me! You owe me big time!"

"You're nimble with a dozer," I recalled, "but can you drive a car? It doesn't have levers or tracks and cleats; just a steering wheel and tires," I ventured. "Cars go faster, too!" He ignored the insult.

"I sweated my ass off for you and her royal nuisance. She owes me, too!"

Now I was laughing: Appear in public with this wonder of the construction world? "Can you dress for the occasion?" He could. "I really wonder," I opined. He insisted. I looked askance. He pleaded. "Well, I *could* use some help getting to the dedication of the new government building, downtown. Her route had been announced, a regular queen's parade. It will be a mob scene. The rest of the day I can handle. Would you like to be my chauffeur for that one occasion?" You bet he would! "You *sure* you can dress appropriately?" He was emphatic. He went to the showers wearing a big grin.

Island preparations continued throughout October. Finally, with our host island thoroughly washed, painted and manicured to the last building, rock and palm tree; with citizens in ecstatic anticipation, we reached the evening of the night before.

At dusk, Jeannie and I set out for the Premier's residence, deep in the countryside on the brow of a low hill. It was a real search in the dark, a pitch black night with no street lights, not even on the Premier's hill. We found his house by following a long line of cars parked on both shoulders of the narrow country road. Dreading the long walk in the dark from the end of the line and up the hill, we were surprised and relieved when the policeman at the foot of the driveway recognized us ("Maja, this way!") and waved us up the driveway. All the way up the dark hill the driveway was decorated on both sides with little candles and paper flags of Great Britain and Antigua. We parked to the right on the front lawn where directed and dismounted. The trade winds had quieted to a whisper, as if on command. We were completely unaware of the Caribbean fairy tale that was about to unfold.

A young Antiguan woman waved us across the driveway with her clipboard. Behind her on the gentle slope of the expansive side yard, we saw a sea of long folding tables with strings of white lights strung above; tables elegantly prepared for dinner. An air field trailer mounted diesel generator could be heard distantly, droning in the back yard. Our guide flipped through pages of guest lists. "Oh yes, Maja, right this way, please." We followed her dutifully, without a clue.

How many tables were there? The following week, Eric told me there were three thousand guests, just over 4% of the island population. There were a *lot* of tables. In the middle of them all stood one extra-long table with extra strings of lights above and extra decorations on the table: clearly the head table. I hoped we would not be too far away to hear the Premier speak, but any table would do. Just to be there was enough!

What we didn't know was that the Premier was hosting six governors, five prime ministers, one chief minister and their wives from all the remaining island colonies and associated states. Most were in the process of emancipation; they soon would be independent nations. Their heads of state would be at the Premier's table this night, anticipating a private audience with the Queen on the morrow. This Caribbean visit of the Queen was, in effect, the swan song of the British Empire. It was little noticed outside the Eastern Caribbean: the 20th century had moved on, but we were witnessing the final tattoo and retreat of a 350 year old Empire.

We also did not know where our young guide was leading us, though she was headed right toward that extra-long table. Our table must be on the far side. Still I did not get it when she stopped at the head table. She was mistaken. She wasn't! There were our place cards, right in the middle of that long table. Above the salt, so to speak!

We stared in wonder at our table mates. We were still trying to get used to the generals, admirals and ambassadors we had hosted to cocktails at our house since June, but these were heads of government! Bless Jeannie! While "the Maja" sat there tongue tied, Jeannie waded in with questions about children, and all wifely things of interest. Guess what?!

All these black potentates turned out to be ordinary mortals- human type mortals! They had the same interests as we lesser mortals: God, family, friends, associates, work, home, and country. The premier of the Turks and Caicos Islands and his wife sat across from us. We had an animated conversation about his government's relations with our sister base at Grand Turk, especially about our friend, Major Vic Flloyd, the Commander of Grand Turk Air Station. The Premier thanked me as we reviewed the occasional support we had provided via the range liner that flew between our islands each week. And on and on. (What didn't I mention? His Minister of Finance, who was caught smuggling cocaine from Haiti in a bongo drum!)

With the Prime Minister's wife, I discussed my developing ability to identify a man's home island by his accent; that on Antigua, our maid could tell me which village! With others, we discussed the sad tendency of island youth not to return to the islands after receiving college degrees in Canada or Great Britain, obtained at great expense to the cash strapped island people. It seemed beneath their newfound educated dignity to return and contribute to the development of their home island. This, the Premier lamented to me on another occasion.

And so it went, late into the evening as we conversed with a table full of latter day George and Martha Washington's; inspired by soft breezes and whispering palms under star filled skies; lubricated by steel band music, Caribbean fare and the free flowing Cavalier Rum of our island paradise.

A fine sipping elixir

The Queen must have arrived during the evening of the Premier's party, because we got first sight of her very early the next morning at her official welcoming ceremony on the Cricket Pitch. She drew a huge crowd to the formalities and walked through the crowd briefly at her departure, greeting citizens as she went. She caught sight of the two of us as Jeannie snapped a picture, giving us a warm smile and wave as she passed. We then departed for home, and I to the base.

Queen Elizabeth at the Cricket Pitch

At ten sharp before my desk, I was presented with a vision of loveliness; well, all right, I exaggerate, but only a little. Right at the appointed moment Dale appeared at my office door. Not only was he clean and cleanly shaven, he sparkled. He had assembled as magnificent a uniform as ever adorned a bulldozer chauffeur. Picture a slightly heavy, slightly balding, early middle aged Irishman bottom to top; white suede shoes, white socks, white starched linen trousers, white belt, ornate white tropical shirt-jacket and a white string tie all topped off with a white linen Irishman's cap. Stunning! I will never know how he assembled that immaculate outfit from the meager resources of our remote island. We were off and running, first to the house to get Jeannie, then on to the new government building, downtown.

As anticipated, it was jammed up with cars and pedestrian traffic down there, but our most excellent chauffeur found a place right adjacent.

Bulldozer fashion, he parked in the middle of the street! Dale, rigidly erect as a king's footman, opened and held the door: we dismounted.

A military uniform is a wonderful thing. As we stepped forward into the pedestrian crowd the multitude parted like the Red Sea. We advanced right through them to the royal microphone, placed twenty feet outside the front door of the new government building, comforted by the fact that Dale was standing fast at the coach - the car - ready, as directed, to expedite our departure.

The new government building was not nearly as ready as were we. It had walls and a roof, OK, but through the broad front windows could be seen unpainted walls, a bare concrete floor and tools of the carpenter's trade. A temporary construction staircase, sans banister, graced an interior side wall: six weeks behind schedule; all quite normal by tropical standards.

There was no time to ponder the island's wonderfully laid back culture. Promptly at eleven, 'Er Royal Rolls Royce rounded another building at our right. So much for English order and the parting of the Red Sea; the Red Sea- the mob- surged forward, engulfing us. As the sea- the mob- calmed to the soft breeze of Sir Wilfred and Premier Bird's welcoming speeches, we found ourselves five back in the crush of humanity. Straining forward to hear 'Er Majesty's first utterances, I heard CLICK, WHIRRRRR!

Turning hard left in the press of humanity, I found myself nose to nose with my favorite and only chauffeur. His assigned post at the car was another seventy feet back. Abandoning his post in haste, he fired his noisy camera right under my left ear. Admonishing him to hang tight at my side, I turned back to hear 'Er Majesty's softly delivered message, punctuated by repeated CLICK, WHIRRRRs. Somewhere in the middle of her encouraging words to the soon-to-be-independent Antiguans, the CLICK, WHIRRRRRings were replaced by a ringing in my left ear. I turned left again with sinking spirits. Sure enough, Dale was gone, not to be found either side or behind. There was no other possibility, except.... I turned to face the Queen, not twenty feet away. In the shifting sea of navy blue suits (British Secret Service?) standing with the Queen, a stark white uniform could not long go unnoticed.

Sure enough, as I watched with deep foreboding, Dale broached from the navy blue suit sea like the great white whale: right alongside, right in the face of, 'Er Royal Blue Eyed Majesty, CLICKing and WHIRRRRing away not a yard from 'Er royal nose. I was shocked; 'Er security folks were stunned. An official Antiguan photographer? A freelancer? 'Er Royal Majesty's documentarian of things royal?

'Er Majesty gave Dale a nervous glance and continued her utterances with a stiff upper lip. Everyone else froze! Then, as quickly as he broached, he submerged in the navy blue suit sea, not to be seen again. At the end of 'Er speech, 'Er Majesty turned toward our right with hasty thanks to the Governor and the Premier and retreated quickly to the security of the Rolls Royce. We fled to the left hoping to beat the traffic (and perhaps Scotland Yard) out of town, but would he be there? He had my keys! No fear. Our coachman stood as stiff as his starched uniform, at his appointed post as if he had never left his station. Not a word was said until the doors were closed and the engine roared to life, masking our uproarious laughter. What star studded brass!

Since we were parked in the middle of the street, Dale merely drifted toward the first corner in a sea of pedestrian traffic, past the left side and beyond the now dedicated building. As he came to the back corner, who should process from right to left across our bow most stately? 'Er Majesty en entourage! Dale took his measure of angle, distance and speed, hove left and dropped into line behind the slow moving and only Rolls Royce in all of Antigua. Bumper to bumper, we were looking down the nape of their necks: 'Er Majesty and Prince Phillip!

What do you do in a Queen's parade? Maintain a stiff upper lip with Royal court dignity, smile and wave to the assembled multitude along the way, as did the queen– all the time trying not to giggle. Decorum was not Dale's strong suit. He struggled stiff-upper-lip-ed-ly with all his might for several long, slow blocks while we acknowledged the crowd and the startled looks on the faces of a scattering of Canadian and English friends and neighbors. Through the open window we heard "Look! There's Al and Jeannie! They're traveling with the Queen!" We acknowledged them with statesmen-like smiles and dignified waves.

Meanwhile, Dale was at the end of his decorum rope. Fortunately, the entourage turned right; Dale hove left and we were out of there, laughing all the way; racing across the island to the house for a late, but celebratory lunch!

*

By evening, I was beginning to regret my decision, limiting Dale to that one event. On the other hand, could we continue to get away with his antics? I really did not want to explain to my commander why I had been thrown off the island. So, for the second evening in a row, Jeannie and I set off in the dark, sans chauffeur; this time for the docks, downtown.

HMY Britannia at dock: a yacht, a vessel of state with length, beam and draft reminiscent of a Caribbean banana boat; an artifact of power, massively constructed of royal blue steel, bright brass, teak and varnished mahogany; a floating museum piece.

HMY Britannia in daylight

Three hundred guests boarded HMY Britannia at nine pm; 296 subjects of the English crown and four Americans: the two commanders and their wives. (There seemed to be extra security this time!) At the bridge mast she flew the national flags of every guest: all the Caribbean colonies and Associated States, Canada and the US. A large union jack graced the stern.

The guest queue wound 'round the first deck and up the stairs to the promenade deck where each guest would be presented to the Queen. The guest line hummed with freely given advice; what to do and especially what not to do upon presentation. "Be sure to bow or curtsy deeply, with great respect. Maintain absolute silence. Do not utter a word, unless she utters first." Period! Could they be serious? They were!

How boring! In line halfway up the stairs, the four Americans held a hasty pow wow. Should Americans follow British rules? What if we didn't? Dick and Bev decided not to bow or curtsy; they would greet her verbally, American style. Conscious of our own heritage, we found no dishonor in simple respect according to Crown custom. It had been some time since the revolution. Let bygones be bygones.

Finally, we reached 'Er Majesty. At the announcement of my name, rank, command and citizenship, I gave 'er a slight bow. Less than a yard separated us; I looked her squarely in the eye- also against protocol, we had been told. "Sorry," I thought, "an American habit."

Under cover of the third deck, close overhead, she wore no hat over her salt and pepper hair, but a many layered filmy dress; long, elegant, pale blue, fully sleeved, suitable to a cool tropical evening at the end of October with a minimal trade wind whispering across the deck. She was indeed royal in appearance, but her eyes could not conceal the hard truth: she was exhausted!

It had been a long day: the formal welcoming at the Cricket Pitch and the dedication of the new government building that morning; followed by a luncheon at the Governor's summer residence out in the country where she met privately with each attending Governor, Prime Minister and Premier of her current and former Caribbean realms and territories. Consider the concentration necessary to keep all their names, their islands and their individual government issues straight! Then the 'round island tour of the hinterland, smiling and waving to numerous village crowds. She ended the tour downtown at a private dinner at Government House with Governor, Sir Wilfred and Lady Jacobs, then returned to Britannia just in time to receive 300 guests! Exhausted, she was, but duty bound.

That I found, was most admirable. Not her great wealth, not her power, not her status, but her indomitable British tenacity: she knew who she was, and that she would be. She owed this courtesy to her subjects and she was standing in there until the last had been honored. Rock solid to the end, she was.

"Cocktails, anyone?"
Queen Elizabeth II and Prince Phillip.

All that and grace, besides. As Jeannie curtsied, the Queen rewarded her with a warm, personal smile and a touch of her hand. Very rare! Nothing was said, but she must have remembered us from that morning at the Cricket Pitch.

We moved on across the deck to enjoy 'Er Majesty's gin and tonic, whilst strolling- promenading- about the promenade deck. Our eyes feasted on every detail of teak plank, brass fittings and varnished mahogany. She and her mistress were two grand imperial ladies!

At a late hour we all were invited to the dockside railing. Below us, the Yacht's drum and bugle corps were on the dock in traditional red coat uniforms, at the ready for a tattoo and retreat. Back and forth, back and forth, in the dim light of a single dock bulb, they marched to the blare of trumpets, the rap of snares and the thump, thump, thump of the bass drum. They moved back and forth, back and forth in centuries old choreography. At the end pride, honor and melancholy battled for control of our emotions as the band played the national anthem of every guest; ending with Rule, Britannia.

All too soon we were waiting on the dock, taking a last long look at this vestige of Empire. The lines were dropped. Britannia slowly moved away from the darkness of the dock into the misty blackness of the harbor. As the deck lights winked out, one by one, as she steamed away, Britannia's hull faded from royal blue to midnight black.

Steeped in pride, honor and melancholy, lost in memories of the Imperial past, we drove home to the realities of our present paradise. I did not know it then, but as the Antiguans were dying to imperial servitude and rising to independent life; so would I, in little over a year, die to self and rise to new life. As the Queen so clearly knew who she was, and to that she was committed; so would I discover and commit to my new, authentic self.

Antiguan Information System
The Major and Jeannie center, shoulder to shoulder, always!

VI. 'Is Majesty's Rain –
November 1977 – November 1978

The voice of the Lord is over the waters, the Lord over mighty waters.
The Lord sits enthroned over the flood; the Lord sits as king enthroned
forever. May the Lord give strength to his people! May the lord bless his
people with peace!

Psalm 29: 3, 10, 11 NRSV

After the Queen's departure, as you might expect, the island quieted down considerably. For most Antiguans, empire was effectively over; final independence was soon at hand, a sobering thought. It meant not only a measure of freedom, but of responsibility. Yet, Caribbean life goes on, Mon, and the snowbirds still would fly.

Like the swallows of Capistrano, the snowbirds land in Antigua every year for the Christmas season, eliciting even more cocktail parties. Of course, we *had* to attend them all. One memorable night, in the Christmas season, 1977, we had three invitations. We regretted one and attended the other two. We hosted our share of parties, as well. Even on a major's paltry salary, the booze was cheap and Antiguan bartenders were happy to work for a few British West Indies dollars per hour. Steel bands? Not so cheap.

You might consider me a lush, all this talk of cocktail parties. The temptation always *was* there, but with the absence of TV, high priced glitzy entertainment, and the frequent absence of a working telephone system (internet and satellite TV were yet in the future), the cocktail party was the essential medium for social dialogue and the negotiation of terms for barter of influence or assistance. I rarely saw anyone really intoxicated (except on British ships), though offered drinks always were strong; the booze was cheaper than the mix. My strategy was graciously to accept a fire breathing gin with a dash of tonic, then top off with tonic all evening. I seemed always to be drinking, but it was only one much thinned down, extended alcoholic drink all night. One must keep a clear head for stealth in this business!

But what I am trying to get to is, the most welcome invitation came on Christmas Eve, 1977. It had nothing to do with a cocktail party. I was working in the office. Harry dropped by around noon as I was beginning to think of the chow hall next door. He said, "Every year on Christmas Eve, Pan Am donates a pickup truck load of beer to the Antiguan laborers. They have a party up at the shops; then take the afternoon off to be with their families. Major, they have asked me on their behalf, to invite you up to their goat water party. I want you to know: never in the history of this base have they invited the commander. This is a first. Will you come up and join them?"

No one could keep me away! We walked up the hill to the shops. In the parking lot the Antiguan workmen had built an open fire on a concrete pad. A regular garbage can was on the fire, full of bubbling (and spicy hot) goat water. Someone handed me a cold beer; I started making the rounds, cocktail party style, shaking hands, conversing with one and all, thanking them for their invitation and their good work.

Goat water? It's an Antiguan Christmas tradition, something between a soup and a stew, depending on the availability of food stock. First you take a garbage can half filled with water which you set to a good boil. Add one goat, suitably chopped up in bite sized pieces, followed by whatever island vegetables and spices may be found. The choice of goat parts is highly flexible, but the spices *must* include a gross of the hottest peppers found on the island. Then, with a fire extinguisher (cold beer) for protection, sample and savor the goat water as long as endurance prevails. Clearly, I was about to be tested.

With the workforce assembled and watching, I savored my first cup full. Wiping tears away, I asked for a refill, much to the admiration and smiling satisfaction of all. It was delicious, but I knew not to ask for thirds. Finally, the party began to break up as the beer and goat water diminished and the laborers' thoughts turned toward home. I expressed my appreciation with hands around and walked back down the hill. It was Christmas Eve. I, too, should be at home.

*

After the New Year's parties, we also had to contend with the parade of British Navy ships that found their way to our warmer waters each winter. The British allow endless drinks aboard, whilst at dock. We attended cocktail parties aboard HMS Fearless and HMS Lyness; plus a Canadian diesel submarine, HMCS Onondaga. The British parties were most humorous, since the junior officers got raging drunk most of the time. (After two drinks, we Americans were referred to as "the colonists!")

HMCS Onondaga turned out to be most technically interesting. Lady Jacobs, late middle aged, had real trouble getting down the ladder to the conn, the center of festivities; but refused to be left on dock or deck. With the help of Governor Sir Wilfred and two slightly inebriated boat officers, she made it to the gin and tonic. At that point Dick Grant, NAVFAC commander, and I retreated to the engine room for a personal tour. Dick had served as XO on the last US diesel submarine, the same class as this sub.

From a historical and cultural point of view HMS Devonshire topped them all, docking at St Johns in the first breath of spring. Governor Sir Wilfred hosted a late afternoon high tea on the front lawn of Government House (his official residence) to honor the ship's senior officers and notables of the island. It was a stately colonial affair that was to end at twilight with a tattoo and retreat by Devonshire's drum and bugle corps. Unfortunately, it started to rain as the corps formed up on the lawn. All of us (perhaps 100 guests, plus the bugle corps) raced to the front porch of Government House as darkness fell. It became one serious, extended downpour!

Government House

Government House was left over from colonial glories: a huge, roughly square two story wood building just like you have seen in the movies, with deep wrap around porches on the bottom floor, large windows everywhere, (pre- A/C, you see) and a huge reception room and adjacent billiard room. Those two rooms, connected by a very wide interior doorway, spanned the entire front half of the first floor.

The crowd was huddled on the dark, expansive porch, backlit by light from interior chandeliers; listening to the rather intense rain and murmuring- "How can we get to the cars?" Sir Wilfred and I were standing together outside on the porch at one of the great reception room windows. The slightly damp Drum Major approached. Sir Wilfred: "I suppose you must cancel the tattoo?"

"Oh, no, Sah! With your permission, we can do it right heah!" His right arm swept in the direction of the two front rooms.

"But that's not possible?!"

Oh yes, Sah! No trouble a' tall!"

With permission, the Drum Major signaled to his men and in 10 minutes or so, all the furniture was removed to the back of the house, even the full sized billiard table! The tattoo and retreat went right ahead. The corps barely fit in the two rooms, touching the walls on the turns. They marched back and forth just as another corps had done on the far more expansive dock at the Queen's departure, as the amazed guests on the porch watched with their noses pressed to the windows. One of those noses was my mother's; a teacher, historian and avid anglophile who visited that week. She was pressed against one of the windows in total fascination. I found out the next morning after breakfast that she spoke to the ship's Captain, inviting his junior officers to an afternoon pool party at our house. (The junior officers had not been invited to Government House the evening before. The grace of my mother would provide.) It was low tea on six hour notice, but a boisterous pool party none the less. Tough duty! Paradise could be exhausting!

*

Ah, but Spring commeth, the snowbirds fly and ships returneth to sea. Antigua seemed to sigh and hunker down. There was work to be done, a Nation to build. Among the government ministries and agencies with which I dealt, a National character of pride and a quiet crescendo of self-reliance seemed to flower – along with a healthy dash of insecurity. Especially, the Royal Antigua Police Force and the firefighters showed a slow but steadily increasing discipline and competence over their 1977 performances. On the base, we were doing quite well, thank you.

Royal Antiguan Police Force in Better Days

Tranquility of order descended upon the base. House cleaning was complete and all knew that fun was encouraged, but it came first *after* mission performance and safety. Tranquility of order is a wonderful thing, as a parade of state side inspectors found. We were consistently getting top ratings. One inspector wrote, "I would be embarrassed to give this perfect rating to Antigua Air Station if I did not know how hard I looked for any shortcomings." I was on a roll: responsible for my beautiful and gracious wife, two lovely daughters, a Caribbean air station and day to day representation of the United States of America to a soon-to-be new nation! I was doing very well, indeed! And so, I thought, all is well in Paradise. I can coast through my second year. Well, yes and no.

It was the year of three Popes. Twice in as many months, Jeannie and I, with the whole Antiguan hierarchy, resident Americans, Canadians and Brits: everyone, received invitations to a Papal Requiem Mass. To my surprise, government ministers en masse, mostly Anglicans, and residents of every nationality filled the Catholic Cathedral to overflow with clearly visible, genuine and heartfelt grief. Still an agnostic, raised without church or faith, I was moved in sympathy with them and with my Catholic wife. On October 16, 1978, John-Paul II ascended to the throne of Peter.

A month later, in the middle of November, I awoke on an unusually cool tropical Saturday morning. On mornings like that, sights and sounds and smells carry with undiminished vigor. I awoke to clanking pots and pans. The sound filtered through the kitchen screens, across the side yard past the tamarind tree and broadcast into the bedroom through open shutters. And there was the crackling sound of grease tap dancing on a hot pan. Jeannie was cooking breakfast under the careful supervision of Mr. Fluff, the house cat. The smell alone- the bacon, not the cat- was a call to action. I pulled on trousers, stood up and grabbed a short sleeved shirt.

Wandering over to the open shutters facing the side yard, I looked out on the crisp, cool morning. Behind the laundry hut, under the Tamarind tree, patches of sunlight and shade were dancing on the lawn to light airs. "Wonderful!" I thought. "If there *was* a God, he'd make a morning like this!"

With the hint of a chuckle, a voice I did not know said, "Why don't you pretend to believe and see what happens?!"

The voice was clear, certainly heard, but there was no one else in the room. It wasn't my own internal voice and that was not just a question, it was a dare! I reasoned, "If that was my brain misfiring, nothing will happen, but if it was God? Maybe there is evidence of God to be had?!"

After eleven years with Jeannie, after several Catholic inquiry and Faith Explained classes, I had converted from a pessimistic agnostic (there probably isn't a God) to an optimistic agnostic (I sure hope there is a God!), but I still did not have any evidence that I could accept.

As *The Voice* suggested, I began to pretend. Tongue in cheek, at breakfast I announced my "faith" to a startled Jeannie. I started to pray up a storm, engaged in churchy talk, actually went to Mass with Jeannie the next day. I was determined to keep my side of the bargain. I did everything I could think of; for two weeks I did. And of course, nothing happened.

In the meantime, Jeannie was planning a last Saturday of the month birthday pool party for Shannon. All Hodges Bay kids would be there, thirty ankle biters. Jeannie and Dorset would handle the inside operation: bake the cake and cookies, supervise and assist clothes changing, sooth and cure six year old battle damage, direct parent and guest traffic.

Pool party, Anyone?

She wanted me to handle the outside operation at the pool: decorate the pool patio, set up tables and chairs, start up the grill, cook and serve endless American hotdogs (bratwurst to brats, I thought) and ice cream, clean up spills, umpire arguments, break up fights, fish drowning kids out of the pool and monitor horse spider traffic.

I mightily resisted the proposed tasks until I realized that even a pretend Christian would be more cooperative. I capitulated. OK, I'll do it. I don't want to, but I will do it! Right! OK! Should be easy!

The invitations were the talk of Hodges Bay. Pool swimming, American hot dogs and ice cream were rare commodities on Antigua. It was not clear who was the most excited, the kids or the parents who were looking forward to an equally rare free afternoon! Meanwhile, I continued to pretend-believe.

The rainy season was late that year, but it arrived with monsoonal vengeance on the Monday before the Saturday party; not so hard, but continuous. Once again, Paradise turned from dust to mud, then puddles, then to random, unauthorized ponds throughout the island. My pretend faith was still going apace, so I began this daily prayer; "Lord, please stop the rain in time for the party." The answer? Sometimes light, sometimes moderate, it kept a-raining! Mid-week I modified the prayer spontaneously; "You know I don't want to be bothered with that party, but come on(!), let's do it for the children!" It kept on a-raining! No let up at all for the rest of the week: truly and typically monsoonal, like the previous year.

Motherly phone calls started Thursday morning and accelerated into Friday, the day before the party; the phone ringing a few times each hour, all day. "Jeannie, the ground is soaked and it's still raining. Aren't you going to cancel the party?"

Jeannie, a prayer warrior for years, responded to every call, "No, don't worry, it won't rain. Bring the children!" Saturday, still raining, it was party time. The motherly calls increased in frequency and grew really anxious. "Jeannie, you *must* cancel the party. The children will catch their death of cold!" You've got to cancel!"

Jeannie's mantra was "Don't worry, it won't rain, bring the children."

During and after breakfast, I sat at the dining room table, gazing through open shutters at the rain dance on the front walk, drinking way too much coffee. It was raining in every direction, across the island and out to sea. The base forecast offered no hope. It would be a very gray day: solid overcast and continual moderate rainfall throughout the Northeast Caribbean. And so it went through the morning, rain and pray, pray and rain. Jeannie also spent the morning praying, but also preparing; and answering frantic phone calls. To one and all she would respond, "Bring the kids, it won't rain." Hodges Bay mothers were beginning to think Jeannie was nuts!

I was *frustrated*! With a background symphony of phones ringing, Jeannie's encouragements to concerned mothers and Dorset's chatter of pots, pans, and laughter, I launched my last appeal. As prayer, it was neither traditional nor very respectful.

"Now look here, Lord! The party is scheduled from 1:00 pm to 4:30pm. I need an hour for the water to run off the lawn and another hour to start the BBQ pit and set up tables and chairs on the pool patio. So if the rain doesn't stop by 11am, I *will* cancel the party. Now come on, Lord, let's do it for the children." It kept a-raining to the tune of a ringing telephone, Jeannie's emphatic encouragements to bring the children and Dorset's laughter.

Decision time was at hand. Jeannie and I stood at the front screen door watching a steady rain, counting down the seconds before my 11:00am deadline: 10, 9, 8,…

I must tell you that I *really knew* what time it was. Are you old enough to remember the Accutron watch, the watch that hummms? At the time, it was the most accurate wrist watch generally available. Mine was set to missile range time which was accurate to six *microseconds*. I knew *exactly* what time it was; 7, 6, 5, 4….3… I pushed open the screen door and stepped across the porch, 2, 1….

At precisely 11:00am Atlantic Standard Time, I stepped onto the front walk. The rain stopped! Precisely as requested in my last, urgent pretend prayer, the rain stopped! Period. Nada! I tried to find a wet spot anywhere on my clothes. Not a drop on me; but in my beautiful, *almost regulation* Air Force boots, I *was* standing in ankle deep water.

All around, on the hills and out in the Atlantic, it was still raining, but not on my yard, not on the five acres around our house! Jeannie, still at the screen door, was treated to quite a spectacle as I danced and splashed around in the water on the front walk: "He did it! He did it! He stopped the rain! He stopped the rain!" Exactly in time to save the party; "let's do it for the children."

After the dance, we went back to another cup of coffee and waited, to the tune of more phone calls and Jeannie's motherly assurances; assurances were needed because it was still raining all over Hodges Bay and out to sea, as far as we could see in every direction and as phone calls affirmed, though not on our yard. We watched and waited the first hour. Sure enough, at the end of it the run-off had---run off. The yard was damp, but there was no standing water (as requested in my last prayer.) Time to go to work!

I hustled about the pool; started the BBQ, arranged the poolside tables and chairs and hung a string of left over Christmas tree lights between two small patio trees. Still, it was raining in all directions as far as eye could see, but not on my yard. I was ready to party at 1:00pm, precisely!

At the bottom of the driveway, cars began arriving, crossing the cattle guard and emerging from the rain, dripping their way up to our shell parking lot, in front. Excited children emerged, walking on dry ground. Worried parents shook their heads and drove back down the driveway, across the cattle guard and into the rain. We began to party at the pool under an overcast sky. It was still raining all around us, but not on our yard.

The kids were oblivious to the concerns of parents, the weather, and to everything else except the swimming pool, American hot dogs and ice cream. Nobody drowned and there was only one minor, if heated, argument. The horse spiders either were intimidated by the crowd of kids or had fled to higher ground. None were seen that day. Meanwhile, mothers kept calling. "Jeannie, it's still raining, it's terrible! The kids will catch their death of cold; shall I come get them?" Jeannie assured them all that it was not raining, not at our house! At our house, the kids were fine, they were having a ball. At their houses? Steady, occasionally heavy rain.

The parents couldn't stand it any longer. They really could not believe Jeannie. They were watching a steady downpour on their flooded yards all over Hodges Bay. A little before 3:00pm, cars began to emerge from the rain, crossing the cattle guard, trailing the last rivulets of rain water that ran off their cars, dripping their way up the driveway. Getting out of their cars on dry ground, looking about in wonder; the parents, all of them, were stunned into silence. They expected to find bone chilled, miserably uncomfortable, drippy nosed children. Instead, they found a bunch of warm, dry and happy kids doing what kids do best.

Place of the watery jig, where parents gather

The parents retreated to the middle of the yard by the tamarind trees, at the end of the front walk. Some could see their own homes through the rain that surrounded us. They gathered in quiet little groups, talking in hushed tones as though in a cathedral. All of them gazed at the sky, at the awesome spectacle that had been standing still above us for four hours, since 11:00am. They saw what I had been watching all afternoon.

From a totally overcast sky, rain squalls processed in train on southeasterly trade winds from across the island. It rained over the

Atlantic, beyond the road. It rained due east on the hill where the Rothsteins lived, to the south at the golf course and over the open field to the west, past the Manchaneel tree and the village of Cedar Grove.

Most unnerving of all was the sight to the southeast, into the teeth of the oncoming squalls. Less than a quarter mile to windward dark clouds were splitting like waves cut by the bow of a ship, passing around our five acres and recombining at our "stern", at the beach road. This had been continuous since 11:00am. Everywhere on the island, out to sea and close at hand, the rain continued. Over us, the sky was solidly overcast, but not a drop fell on our yard all afternoon.

By 3:30pm, the children were 'et out, played out, and worn out. Mothers got them redressed in the house, donning raincoats for the trip home; said their thanks, took a last look at the sky and headed for home, driving down the driveway, across the cattle guard and into the steady rain. Finally, only our close friend, Sheila Rothstein and her two children, Jonathan and Etien remained. While Jeannie, Sheila and Dorset straightened up the house, I attacked the pool patio.

This was not the fun part: pick up the trash, douse the BBQ, collect and put away BBQ tools, reorganize tables and chairs, etc., etc., etc. Last of all, I took down that string of lights, strung from patio tree to patio tree; placed the string on the glass top patio table by the pool gate. I stood there by the table, surveying my handiwork, but what was that faint hissing sound?

Looking up to windward, toward that hissing sound, now becoming a roar; a heavy rain squall was advancing across the yard, straight at me! I grabbed the string of lights and turned for the white picket fence, backhanding the pool gate closed as I bolted for the house. In the middle of the backhand, I saw my wrist watch. The deluge hit me at that moment, precisely 4:30pm, precisely at the party ending time specified in my pre-party prayer.

I ran on into the house soaked and laughing. Every detail of my frustrated demand prayer had been answered, precisely, to the second! "Come on, Lord, let's do it for the children!" The rain continued for several more days, now even on our yard.

"Why don't you pretend to believe and see what happens?" That party was a happening! At supper, watching the rain from the safety of the dining room table, Jeannie and I had a lot to think about over one more cup of coffee.

*

Years earlier, in January 1974, Jeannie and I were stationed in Alaska: she and one year old Shannon staying in Fairbanks; I commuting weekly (by car or by Alaskan Railroad) to remote Clear Air Force Station. I hit psychological bottom that month. Twenty three hours of darkness each day, 50 degrees below zero; working quick turn shifts and family separation can do that to the best of us. Alaskan suicides spike in deep winter every year. Somewhere I had read, *"Ask and you will receive, search and you will find, knock and the door will be opened."* I had searched for years, but had never asked. In anguish, I prayed at bedtime.

You know that old joke where the guy prays, "Is anyone up there?" It was that kind of prayer. I needed help and I just wanted the truth. From childhood and about all things, I had only ever wanted the truth. Evidence and truth were hard to come by, but that night I slept peacefully for the first time in several months. I asked. There was nothing else to do. "Anybody up there?!"

Now almost five years later and before the party, I still had no evidence that I could accept. Evidence of God was critically important to me. I just wanted the truth, and I was not going to declare a faith I didn't have. Whatever it was, the truth was the truth. "OK, God, is you is or is you ain't?" I was sure that I had not controlled the weather that day.

How 'bout, "I AM?" Indeed, Jeannie and I had a lot to think about over that last cup of coffee.

VII. Take the Reins, O My King – Christmas 1978

All of us are interested in what Heaven may think... so most of us are interested in "signs." We get them in many ways...through what we read...through what others say...(through) what we see. "God speaks quietly, but He gives us all kinds of signs. In retrospect, especially, we can see that He has given us a little nudge through a friend, through a book, or through what we see as a failure---even through 'accidents.' If we remain alert, then slowly they piece together a consistent whole, and we begin to feel how God is guiding us."

Pope Benedict, XVI

T he following morning, Sunday, I was standing in the living room looking out at the front lawn and the brick walk where on the previous morning I had danced my soggy jig in ankle deep water. I was praying again; but this time, there was no pretending. My prayer wasn't particularly pious, but it *was* decisive. "Alright, Lord, you got me with that one. I guess I should join a church, probably Catholic for family unity and all that, but I won't join any church 'till you tell me which one."

My reverie of remembrance continued for a few minutes, watching the rain dance on the front walk. Still lost in thought, I wandered back through the short hall and entered the bedroom. Immediately on the right, there was a small lamp table with built in bookcases just beyond. I scooped up a paperback that was on the table, let it fall open in my hand, looked down and read, "Your spiritual home is the Roman Catholic Church." The book was Christ Among Us, popular at the time.

"Good enough for me," I said aloud.

Father Powers was on my protocol list, so from my office Monday morning, I called for an appointment, not mentioning the subject 'til walking through his office door. This was going to be a *big* decision. Nervous, I blurted out, "What do I have to believe to become a Catholic?"

He was caught totally off guard; pushed back in his seat. So I sat down and gave him the short version of my weekend experiences. He was still struggling; just how best should he answer the question? "What if we went line by line through The Creed (which I had heard many times before without making it my own) and I could agree to every line? Would that be enough?" It would be sufficient; we sat there in his office for nearly an hour, discussing every line, every belief, one by one. After what had happened over the weekend, I understood The Creed as never before. It was easy to commit. From my years with Jeannie and a number of Faith Explained courses taken over that time, I had an adequate intellectual understanding of what I was accepting. We arranged for me to be baptized early in the New Year, 1979.

It was only the first week of December. Why wait? I was joining a church definitely not to the liking of my parents and my mother's family. There might be trouble. There definitely *would* be trouble! (At fifteen, my father had taken me aside and advised, "…never marry a Catholic and it would be best if you never dated one." One of the dark, scandalous secrets kept hidden in the family was that his father, my grandfather was a Catholic convert. I only found that out well after my marriage to Jeannie and my grandfather's death.)

Dad had died five years previously, so I would explain my choice (God's choice) to my mother during our Christmas visit in Houston. I was determined not to live my life according to family prejudices. Father Powers assured me I could safely wait, even if the plane crashed and we never made it back to Antigua; "You already have the baptism of desire."

Yet, within a week I began to have doubts; not about my experiences or decision, but about me, my worthiness. What if I didn't measure up? Could I come this far and still be lost? (These days, I know where that doubt comes from, but at the time, it really bothered me.)

After a few days, and with the rain finally gone!, I found myself standing outside, half way down the front walk where I had splashed my victory jig; staring at the North Atlantic sky. Sort of staring at the sky, I should say. The branches of the twin tamarind trees marking the end of the walk and the steps down to the shell parking lot blocked much of the sky. There was an opening however, roughly rectangular, like a movie screen. I began to see a "skit" acted out as fair weather clouds drifted left to right across the "screen."

The first cloud that caught my attention seemed to confirm my fears: it was long, narrow, serpentine; cobra-like, ready to strike. It stopped and remained poised at the left. If that was not enough, on the right side of the "screen" a standing cloud formed in place in the shape of a white robed man with long, gray hair; his back was toward me. I was horrified! Then, I relaxed. "He" was not showing rejection, but was standing between me and the serpent. As soon as I understood this, both clouds drifted off behind the right hand tree.

I was still watching the now empty "screen" when the smallest of standing clouds, hardly a white dot on the blue sky, formed in the middle. Slowly, holding to the center of "the screen," it grew, taking the form of a classic Valentine heart, except it was a string outline, empty in the middle. As the heart expanded into the tree branches all around and disappeared, *That Voice* with a hint of a familiar chuckle, said "My heart is big enough for everyone, even for you!"

*

In Houston, we discovered a large Catholic church in my mother's neighborhood. We decided on the midnight mass, Christmas Eve, 1978. The church attendant urged us, "be sure to get here at least an hour early;

the church will be packed." Have you ever tried to wake up two sleepy little girls and get them into the car around 11:00pm? You will not be surprised to learn that we arrived precisely at midnight. To say the church was packed would hardly be sufficient.

The whole church; pews, center aisle, side aisles, right and left wall aisles, back wall, the vestibule; the whole church - a proverbial sardine can. Jeannie, carrying two year old Katie, was the last one in. She squeezed and pushed through the outer door, barely into the vestibule. Carrying our six year old Shannon (both girls were asleep), I was left teetering on the outer threshold. Literally! That is where I was, and doing what I was doing! I finally got my balance, heels still on the threshold of the outer vestibule door.

Prayer time! "Lord, the children can't see, much less hear!"

Immediately, I saw a bald headed usher, way down front in the center aisle, right in front of the altar. He started elbowing and pushing his way up the center aisle. I knew that I knew that he was coming to us, don't ask me how. Quickly, I lost sight of him in the crush of humanity; but a few minutes later he appeared at the inner door to the church proper, *looking right at me across the crowded vestibule*. I was still standing heels on the outer threshold. He elbowed his way straight at me, across the vestibule. Nose to nose; he shouted over the noise of the crowd, "I have four seats down front! Would you like them?" We would!

He turned without another word, elbowing and pushing his way through the vestibule crowd with Jeannie and me in hot pursuit, still carrying the sleeping children. Across the vestibule, into the brightly lit, wonderfully decorated main church, left through the back wall crowd, right along the crowded left wall, all the way to the front wall of the church; right turn and up on the altar stage, elbowing and pushing all the way.

There were two rows of folding chairs set up on the altar stage alongside the altar, all chairs occupied- except for the four chairs nearest the altar. We were two steps away from the right rear corner of that altar! Thank you Jesus! The children *definitely* could see and hear from there! Our usher, standing between Jeannie and me, motioned for us to sit. Quickly, I put Shannon down and turned to thank him. *There was no one there!* Nor did Jeannie see him leave. I spent the entire mass rubber necking, looking for the man; never saw him again.

That whole event begs questions that I have never been able, definitively, to answer. How could I have seen him so clearly in the crush of humanity between the outer vestibule threshold and the altar of that very large church? How is it that at the end of my one liner prayer, he responded instantly, moving toward us, or that I could have known so surely that when he started to move he was coming for us? How could he have seen us from his post down front immediately after we arrived? And there was no time for a message to be sent forward to him. Cell phones were still in the future. How could he know so positively that in the ten or fifteen minutes it took to reach us and then get back to the altar stage through that packed church, no one else would take those seats? There were many people nearby. They must have seen those seats. Why didn't someone take them? Finally, how could he disappear instantly? He was right beside, between us! Who, or what, was he?

*

After Christmas, we flew commercial to Melbourne, Florida, transferred to a USAF C-141 and flew home to Antigua. At age 38, I was baptized by Father Powers, receiving baptism, confirmation and first communion – the body and blood of the King. Jeannie witnessed; the NAVFAC commander, Dick Grant and his wife Beverley, sponsored. I took the baptismal name Cornelius with good reason.

In Caesarea there was a man named Cornelius, a centurion of the Italian Cohort.... (Acts 10:1) We had parallel stories. He was a commander assigned in a foreign country. He would have been in command of between 100 and 200 souls, as was I. His family was with him, "a devout man who feared God with all his household." He heard a heavenly message and responded with obedience. He stood at the threshold, converted and was baptized. Finally, He and his wife received the Holy Spirit, *The Spirit of Unity.* Now, I also was at the threshold; soon I would be at home in the Spirit, living in *The Spirit of Unity.*

Cornelius, Centurion

VIII. Reign of the Paraclete – February 1979

When the day of Pentecost had come…suddenly from heaven there came a sound like the rush of a violent wind, and it filled the house…. Divided tongues, as of fire…appeared among them…. All of them were filled with the Holy Spirit and began to speak in other languages, as the Spirit gave them ability.

   Acts 2:1-4 NRSV

After the girls left the supper table; Jeannie, with a little difficulty in choosing words said, "Something really strange happened to me, recently. I really don't understand it, but here, read this book." Her demeanor was a little strange. My first thought was, "she is trying to tell me she has some horrible, life threating disease." She went on to explain, whatever *it* was, was a good thing, she just did not have the words to describe it. Her urging was so strong; I went to the living room and started to read.

The book, <u>Fire on the Earth</u> by Ralph Martin, a 99 page paperback book, was written to describe his experience in the early days of what was coming to be known as the Charismatic movement. I read 'till bedtime, which was quite early since we were very tired. We crawled into bed right after the kids went to sleep, maybe as early as 9:00pm. Jeannie went right to sleep. Thoroughly engrossed, I kept a-reading, reaching finis after ten. The book was amazing, especially the part about something he called "being filled with the Holy Spirit." I was familiar with the "Acts of the Apostles" chapter two; there was a connection here, somewhere. Reflecting a bit, I prayed "Lord, it's probably much too soon, now; I've only been a Christian for a couple of weeks, but whenever you think I'm ready, I want this." With that, I slept, but not for long!

In the middle of the night, I awoke with a start. I was already praying aloud, speaking rapidly in a strange language. Fully awake, immediately I knew what was happening. I couldn't move. Paralyzed (!), but not afraid. While the audible tongues continued, a quick mental inventory revealed that I could think, hear, voice the tongues (though I had no control of that), feel, and move my eyes; but could not move my head, arms, legs or torso. There was the sound of wind roaring through the house (it was a calm night; the trade winds were nearly still) and I felt like I was burning up. Then I noticed a moderate pressure on the middle of my back and behind my knees, as though a baby, being cradled in someone's arms. This went on for what seemed like a couple or three minutes; then, the tongues started tapering off. I tried to keep it going, but I had no control over it. It just went of its own accord. Then it was over; the tongues, the paralysis, the wind, the heat, the pressure on my back and legs, all were gone. I had full faculties. With a thank you "Our Father, who art..." and a big smile, I slept the night away.

In the morning, I gave a full account. Jeannie was delighted; her experience of this had been similar. Only my summary explanation was new. "It was as though He held me in His arms while the Holy Spirit re-wired my computer!" Perhaps not theologically eloquent, but consider my technical background; it was a pretty good analogy.

It was about this time Jeannie and I chose to commit ourselves to a life in obedience to God. (As a college senior, I had committed to a life of service, in gratitude. I did not know God, so my gratitude and desire to serve focused on country. It was the highest calling I knew. My father had been a B-29 radio operator in '45 and the college had an ROTC detachment. My path seemed clear. I committed myself to the Air Force.)

This new commitment was similar, but required an unconditional stance. Whatever God wanted from us, we wanted for ourselves. "Lord, just let us know!" Mind you, the commitment was an event, but learning to live that way still remains a trial and error, lifelong process! As you will see, obedience, sometimes blind, can be a real pain. Still, we soon learned that our recent experience of the Holy Spirit had removed a certain spiritual blindness. Miracles became a part of our weekly, if not daily, life. Things were happening of which we had not ever dreamed; had never noticed.

In the tender compassion of our God the dawn shall break upon us, to shine on those who dwell in darkness and the shadow of death, and to guide our feet into the way of peace.

Luke, Chapter 1:78,79 NRSV

Sir Luther Wynter, left center, looking at camera
Lady Wynter, rear center, wearing sunglasses

IX. Reign of Peace – Winter/Spring 1979

Peace be within your walls, and security within your towers.
For the sake of my relatives and my friends I will say, "Peace be within
you." For the sake of the house of the Lord our God, I will seek your
good.   *Psalm 124: 7-NRSV*

S till, we had a base to run, a missile and space tracking mission to accomplish, and I had to joust with a number of government and commercial operatives, including the Canadian government and their contractors. The Canadians were planning the construction of a new air terminal at Antigua on the very land that Dale had cleared for the Queen in '77. And of course, they planned it right on top of our long established power and communications easement, i.e. our deeply buried cables. To ice the cake, they demanded we move our cables out of their way at our own expense. Not a chance! We were amenable to the move, but equally amenable to our current easement. They would have to pay us for the move. But it was not in their budget! I will spare you the details of the ensuing two month harangue. They paid.

Besides, there is a much bigger tale to tell. As in every year, we hosted the annual radar conference in February. This was a big deal on the Eastern Test Range; an annual gathering from Cape Canaveral, Patrick AFB and the range bases of all the radar managers, engineers, technicians, operators and logisticians, sixty or more of them attending each year; many of them were National experts in their disciplines. So?

Let me share with you the opening two paragraphs of my welcoming speech, given 27 February 1979.

"Good morning and welcome to our island paradise. During the last eleven days, Antigua has run out of diesel fuel, run out of propane, run out of gasoline, run out of hospital oxygen, suffered island wide power outages ranging from 14 hours to five days and more, jailed the opposition leader for alleged financial crimes committed during his recent administration, reacted to a yellow fever scare in Trinidad and jailed the two Marxist leaders, Tim Hector and Joshua Samuels.

At NAVFAC and Antigua Air Station we have cut off and now restored most of the non-mission electrical power, lost the air conditioning in our best barracks (where some of you are staying), padlocked the Satellite club for the benefit of Pan Am auditors, and the Navy Exchange is running out of food and medicine. Given the circumstances, you can understand how greatly we appreciate your good humor and patience; you are indeed welcome here."

How could this be? There were two power plants on the island, the government run all-island power plant (not totally reliable, but normally adequate) and the Air Station power plant that also supplied NAVFAC. (Harry's power plant was super reliable, protecting the mission of both American bases.) Both plants generated electric power with a long line of high capacity diesel generators. Our weak link however, was fuel supply. West Indies Oil Company (WIOC) was the all island fuels distributor. They provided fuel at a respectable, long established rate. During the late Fall, someone stopped paying the ultimate crude oil supplier, Texaco, for fuel deliveries. Of course, we were not told. Nor was it ever clear who was at fault, the government or WIOC. Life goes on in Paradise. "Jus now, Mon." Steel bands still would play, trade winds still would blow, palm trees still would wave and rum still would be cheap. "Not to worry, mon!"

West Indies Oil Company's Antiguan Refinery

Texaco officials were not amused by this exercise of relaxed tropical character. After a gentlemanly pause, they cut off all crude shipments. And again, of course, we were not told. Life goes on in Paradise, mon. Steel bands still would play, trade winds still would blow, palm trees still would wave and rum still would be cheap. On-island diesel storage tanks began to run low. The first hint of trouble came when Harry appeared at my office. "Fuel deliveries to the power house have been running a little short for several weeks. Their invoices show full truckloads, but on every trip, someone is tampering with the truck gauges and liberating a few barrels of diesel."

That was fixed with an advisory to Eric and another to our supplier--- we had noticed! Still we did not have the full picture. We assumed the truck driver was making a little extra BWI (British West Indies currency, pronounced Bee Wee) on the side. However....

Days later, the supplier called to notify me that regrettably, "so sorry Maja; the cost of diesel fuel has doubled." Harry had a conniption fit over that assault on his budget. This problem, too, was mine to solve – not quite so easy as before, but there had to be a way. After a flurry of phone calls to Down Range Affairs and the fuels office at Patrick; to Military Sea Transport Service (MSTS) at Port Canaveral and MSTS HQ at Norfolk, the plan was set. I called WIOC.

"Good morning, Mr. G_____, Major Hughes. How are you? Yes, fine. Regarding your new price for diesel, we did a little checking. Military Sea Transport Service can deliver a monthly shipload of diesel from Port Canaveral to High Point Pier – right to our doorstep, so to speak - at a savings. If we ask them, deliveries can begin in four to six weeks. Our diesel tanks are nearly full now, so we – sorry to say- we will have no need for further deliveries after today– but let me assure you, we deeply appreciate our association with you over the last 20 years."

(After a year and a half of international verbal jousting at my quasi-diplomatic post, I, like my friend Benny, was getting pretty good at this game. I knew *just* what to say.)

The next day, Harry called, shouting above the drone of those big diesels. "The delivery truck – a *full* delivery truck- is up here at the power plant topping us off at the usual price."

As we long had learned to expect, WIOC did not notify us of the "reduction" in price, they just did it. By now, we were suspicious, anticipating the worst; Harry kept our tanks topped to the brim. The worst didn't take long to arrive. Deliveries stopped all together- without notice.

The island power plant and telephone system shut down --- the island's diesel tanks were dry. And still, no one paid Texaco. "Jus now, mon." Steel bands still would play, trade winds still would blow, palm trees still would wave and rum still would be cheap. "Not to worry, mon."

Both bases went to minimum mission power and we shut down half the generators. After we achieved an irreducible minimum, Harry estimated we could continue mission operations for at least two months, perhaps a few weeks more. We also parked half our truck fleet. I notified my commander and put MSTS on standby, ready to deliver. As everything electrical (and gasoline-able) ground to a halt off base, a holy quiet descended across the entire island.

Who needs electricity?

Man cannot live on bread alone, but Antiguans can live without electric power, lights and telephones. They were accustomed and well prepared for power and telephone outages lasting many hours, even a couple of days. At home we, too, had learned to be ready. Out came the candles, the little glass chimney candle lamps, the oil lamps, note paper and envelopes.

Communication among friends, neighbors and business associates in Hodges Bay (most often invitations to tea or cocktail parties) continued apace by hand delivered notes, formal and informal. Since nearly everyone lived within a two mile strip along the Atlantic beach, notes were delivered by Shank's Mare, in person or by a family runner or someone who was "going over that way, anyway." Most often, of course, a friendly face with a note at the door elicited an immediate informal invitation to remain awhile for quickly made tea or other liquid libation, and perhaps pastry or cheese and crackers, to boot. The social life of Hodges Bay, always active, exploded into hyper activity.

Other than the occasional enthusiastic steel band, happy voices and whispering trade winds, the silence was profound. Missile launch rates were down at the same time, the base was running smoothly (and quietly on minimum power) and road noise was much reduced. We had been transported back to the early Victorian era. Community thrived joyfully, with little distraction. These were our most joyful, peaceful days in Paradise. Whoever had neglected to pay Texaco was to be congratulated!

Commander Clowns at peace
Lt. Commander Dick Grant, left; "The Major", right

Regrettably, Texaco returned us to the 20th century by solving the problem. They parked a ship load of crude oil just off the mouth of St. John's harbor, not far from the WIOC fuel dock. They let it sit there for two weeks, swinging at anchor like a hypnotist's watch on a watch fob in full sight of half the island population; moving to and fro; away from the fuel dock on falling tides, toward the fuel dock on rising tides; hypnotically slow, rhythmic; so near, so far, so near…. Downtown, the political pressure became unbearable. After a two week dance on the anchor chain, bills were paid and the ship moved to the WIOC fuel dock. I thanked MSTS for standing by; life in Paradise continued to delight. "Jus now, mon." Steel bands still would play, trade winds still would blow, palm trees still would wave and rum still would be cheap. "Not to worry, mon."

*

While all that was going on, it was the same spring in which we, at home, were getting used to living in the Spirit. Our eyes were opened, and miracles abounded. We were in Spiritual high gear! Life itself, and everyday events seemed routinely miraculous. We can't remember them all, but four examples will suffice.

One night, early on, we awoke to little Katie's crying; really more screaming than crying. Jeannie jumped up and ran to the front bedroom (Mom's do that!) I rolled over; pulled the pillow over my head (Dad's do that!) Right through the pillow I heard Jeannie yelling, "Al, Katie is burning up with fever! Go get the thermometer!"

I yelled back, "Where is it?" (Dads *always* do that!) How are dads supposed to know where mom puts everything?

"It's in the medicine cabinet. Hurry!"

I rolled out, stumbled into the bathroom; opened the cabinet. Of course, it *wasn't* there, but I knew better than to ask again. In the midst of the frantic search, my mind turned to the worst scenario. "I may have to race to the base and call in a medivac chopper from Roosevelt Roads, Puerto Rico. The chopper will have to refuel at arrival, it's too far for a round trip. I'll have to wake up Dennis Nanton and roust out the Aerodrome fuels crew in the middle of the night!" It will be the talk of the island! I'll be explaining this to higher headquarters for weeks!" Moments later, I saw the thermometer on the little night table by the window. Bolting out the bathroom door I announced, "Found it!"

"Never mind!"

By now, I was at her side. "Wa da ya mean, 'Never mind,' you said she was burning up! What happened? What did you do?"

"Shusssh! I laid hands on her, prayed, and the fever just left. She's cool and sound asleep! She's just fine." And she was. We went back to bed and slept soundly through the night.

Maybe a couple of weeks later, another healing occurred. For some time, Patches had been sick and getting sicker. Jeannie and Dorset managed to get him in the car for a trip to the vet. (The vet lived at the end of a dirt road. There was a time in the rainy season when I had to send some guys from the base with a four wheel drive pickup to haul Jeannie back to dry land.)

As the vet approached the car to render aide, Patches suddenly sat up on the back seat and gave a remarkable imitation of a howling mad, rabid dog; though rabies did not exist on the island. The vet took one look at the multitude of teeth, the flood of saliva, and Patches' less than helpful attitude; backed away and said he could not help.

Patches in better days

So whatever Patches had; progressed. Then one day, Patches was found lying in the weeds, clearly dying. Jeannie called over a passel of kids playing in the yard; Shannon, Katie, Sheila's Jonathan and Etien and two, Isabel and Lupi, from a house over the back fence. They all laid hands on Patches, gasping for life (the dog, not Jeannie and the kids.) After a couple of minutes of prayerful "treatment", Patches got up most casually and ambled away. Months later, when we left the island for good, he was still in good health and on duty in front of the house.

(The father of Isabel and Lupi was a LIAT pilot. He provided us a steady supplyof Dutch cheese from St. Maarten Island. In exchange, his family enjoyed a place on the protocol list, with access to the Satallite Club bar, cafe, and free movies in our open air theatre.)

I got involved in another kind of "casual miracle" after power was restored to the Island. I had promised to go home for lunch with Jeannie, but around 11:00am Eric called me over at the base. (Yes, Antiguan phones were working again.) I was needed down town right away. I called Jeannie for a kitchen pass. "Pray first," she said.

"Wha da ya mean, pray first? Pray for what?" (For forgiveness for breaking a lunch date?)

"Before you leave the base, pray for a parking place. I pray before I drive down town and I always have a parking place, right where I am going!"

"You're kidding!"

"Am not! Try it!"

Parking down town always was a challenge. The streets were laid out in the 17th and 18th centuries; many still cobblestone. Admiral Lord Nelson would have been right at home. St Johns was designed for horse carriages, not automobiles where half of the National population lived. The approach to government offices in the old colonial customs house at the base of High Street, right at the old inner harbor dock, was the worst! At the noon hour, it would be the worst of the worst. I tried Jeannie's plan, praying as I rolled out the front gate of the base.

How 'bout that! Arriving at the foot of High Street in bumper to bumper traffic, I pulled into the one and only open parking slot, right under Eric's office window! Not only that, but for weeks thereafter, any time I went down town, a single slot always was available right where I was going, *if I prayed in a request before leaving the base.* The only time this didn't happen, I forgot to pray until I was halfway to town. I prayed then; however....

It was jammed up as usual down High Street; not a parking place in sight. I prayed up an apology, asked if I might please have a reasonable parking place, and began a slow circle around the block creeping, stopping and easing forward, in bumper to bumper gridlock. Returning to High Street two blocks up from the harbor, I could see that there were no open spaces; but as I finally reached the bottom of High Street, a car backed out right in front of me, right under Eric's window. It seemed like God was making sure with these little gifts that we didn't forget his Presence.

Draw your own conclusions. All this and much more happened those last months.

Jeannie continued to have similar experiences until we left Antigua. During our last couple of months, she had a habitual rider, a little old non-practicing Jewish lady who lived in a dead end lane behind the house. The old lady was alone, somewhat bitter, generally depressed and had no transportation. Jeannie befriended her and after a few weeks the old lady perked up. She started telling all the women in Hodges Bay, "Be sure to go downtown with Jeannie. She always has a parking place." Soon, others joined Jeannie's "carpool" and saw the truth of this. It became the talk of Hodges Bay. Finally, the old dear confided to Jeannie a dream.

She had never been a dancer, but in the dream she was sitting alone against the wall of a dance hall watching others dance. A handsome man, dressed in a white suit came up to her; invited her to dance. They danced the night away.

Jeannie interpreted the dream for her. It was Jesus inviting her to the dance. Jeannie continued to witnessed to her the best she could, but we were about to leave the Island for good. So, she hooked the lady up with a nun living on the island. When we left, they were still talking; the old dear was well on her way. We pray that she became a messianic Jew.

In this life, no one can remain in Paradise forever; neither professionally, nor spiritually. Once again, a change of command ceremony rolled around; only this time, we were leaving. I was heartsick, leaving all our base and island friends; the tropical breeze, the swaying palms, the lovely beaches and crystal waters, the steel bands, the base and island community that we grew to love and the best, most fulfilling job I ever had: I fell into a daze of sudden depression. The command was relinquished, the last good bye cocktail party was enjoyed, hugs all around, and the inevitable arrived. There was a C-141 holding on the ramp, engines idling, waiting for Jeannie, waiting for Shannon, waiting for Katie, waiting for me.

For the last time we went to the airstrip to board, bound for Patrick. I was devastated. And there, at the edge of the tarmac, lined up in the best military formation they could muster, was my ragtag army of self-named range rats, the entire civilian crew of Pan Am and RCA– civilian employees all– doing their best to stand at attention. At a command, they saluted our passing by, leaving me on the edge of tears. From the top of the loading stair, I rendered them, rendered Paradise a parting salute, and entered the aircraft.

X. Reins and Pains of Obedience –
1983 – 1985

As a rule, religious persons generally assume that whatever natural facts connect themselves in any way with their destiny are significant of the divine purpose with them. Through prayer the purpose, often far from obvious, comes home to them, and if it be 'trial,' strength to endure the trial is given. Thus at all stages of the prayerful life we find the persuasion that in the process of communion energy from on high flows in to meet demand, and becomes operative within the phenomenal world. So long as this operativeness is admitted to be real, it makes no essential difference whether its immediate effects be subjective or objective. The fundamental religious point is that in prayer, spiritual energy, which otherwise would slumber, does become active, and spiritual work of some kind is effected really.

William James, Philosopher, Psychologist
Varieties of Religious Experience, (1902)

Three years later, we were back at Patrick AFB and Cape Canaveral for the third time. Jeannie and I went wild after Antigua – in a religious sense – getting involved simultaneously in every church lay ministry we could find; always eager to do more. Father O'Toole finally got us under control. He said, "I only want you to do one thing for me (as pastor of the on-base Patrick AFB Parish), but do it well." We tried, getting our list of activities down to two: lay Eucharistic ministers (assisting with communion at mass) and the organization and leadership of the Patrick AFB Youth Group.

At work, I was still on a roll, now returned to the center stage of my career, the Air Force Eastern Test Range. In the 1960's (a Captain) I managed doppler radar development for the range; in the early 70's (newly a Major) I managed world-wide operations of the Space Detection and Tracking System (SPADATS) as a Senior Director of the Space Defense Center, NORAD Cheyenne Mountain Complex. In the late

70's (a senior Major) I returned to Patrick for a short tour at Downrange Affairs in preparation for the command at Antigua. From Antigua, we moved to HQ Systems Command (then a Lt. Colonel) to conduct long range planning for the command's Nationwide test and evaluation ranges and test assets; then home again for the third time at Patrick to conduct technical planning and requirements analysis for Cape Canaveral and all the range stations; I was in line to become the Director, Plans and (who knows?) perhaps eventually Commander of the entire range.

Then I made the big mistake. O, my beloved Air Force! NEVER, NEVER, NEVER attempt a bargain with God. He holds *all* the cards and the future as well.

Promotion time came again, promotions made by an anonymous board of senior officers meeting in seclusion to review the records of a thousand or so candidates. I don't know what I was thinking, perhaps trying to influence the odds. Dumb! "Lord, if you want me to stay in the Air Force, promote me. If they don't promote me, I'll take that as a sign you want me to retire." (I had reached the 20 year mark for active duty, eligible to retire; but also eligible to serve another eight years.)

Late fall of '82 I was passed over. O, my beloved Air Force! I cannot leave you. Eight more years to go! I did what any blue blooded American boy would do. I reneged.

I put the bargain out of my mind. I pretended there was no deal. I argued with God. I argued with me. I engaged in many a contorted rationalization, desperately looking for a way out. You must understand my psychological state. After twenty wonderful, fulfilling years as a professional Air Force officer; still looking forward to more challenges, psychologically I was the Air Force and the Air Force was me. I knew no other life; I wanted no other life. I was desperate to stay to the legal limit, eight more years with my beloved Air Force. And I again would be considered for promotion for two more years. I only….

Early in the new year, I came to face myself. A deal is a deal, especially with God; the God who already had gone to the trouble of revealing Himself, had done so much for us. It was the day of decision.

My secretary, my palace guard at the door, had taken the day off. Behind her desk, she had a typing table set against the wall, holding the only typewriter in the room (PC's were still in the future.) I sat down and typed a resignation letter to my Commander, Colonel Marvin Jones; requested retirement. I swiveled around to the left in the secretary's chair, threw both feet up on her desk and leaned back, left elbow on the desk; staring at the letter held in my right hand. I said, half aloud, "Al, are you really going to sign this letter?" The secretary's phone rang.

It was Marion, my secretary at Air Force Systems Command, up in Maryland. We had not spoken in maybe eighteen months, since I returned to Patrick. We engaged in standard chit chat. "How are you doing? How's the weather? (Cold and rainy in Maryland, warm and sunny in Florida) What ever happened to old so and so? Etc., etc., etc." I had not moved; feet on desk, letter in right hand, staring at *that* letter while talking. *Staring at that letter, while talking.*

In the middle of a sentence, Marion's voice dropped an octave to a very masculine voice, *That Voice*, and said, "I know you are trying to make a difficult decision, and I want you to go ahead and do it." Her voice went right back to normal.

"Marion, did you hear that? Do you know what you just said?" Told her what I was doing and told her what she (*That Voice*) had said.

She responded, "Oh, my God!"

"Yes, I think so." There was little more to say. We finished the conversation; I signed the letter. Active duty would terminate on 31 May 1983.

Consider: I was taking an action totally against my will. O! My beloved Air Force! Not knowing what came next: I had a family to support and no job prospects. I had never looked around to consider alternatives; why should I? I was the Air Force! What I had done terrified me! O! My beloved Air Force! O, my God! Obedience is painful! *Thy will be done on earth....*

He did not leave us orphaned. At the start of spring, clock still ticking down toward fearsome June, on a Sunday, Jeannie and I were at mass. During communion I held the cup over at the left side of the congregation, serving a line of parishioners. When she was still two back in the line, I recognized a neighbor who lived on base a block away from us. She looked devastated.

Everything about her face said fear and trembling, horror and depression, deep dread to the threshold of hopelessness. Then she was right before me. At the instant she touched the cup, something went from me to her. It was like a breath, a short exhale, a launch of energy, taking no longer than it would take to say "Huh!" It was not my lungs; it went from my entire body, a movement of Spirit. It was Power.

Perhaps you know the gospel passage. Jesus is in a crowd. A woman touches his robe. *Then Jesus asked, "Who touched me?" When all denied it, Peter said, "Master, the crowds surround you and press in on you." But Jesus said, "Someone touched me; for I noticed that power had gone out from me."* Lk 8: 44-46 NRSV

The event revealed that He was in me, and I in Him, as Scripture promises all who follow Him. (John 14:18-23 NRSV) He was with me and using me in my obedience. My fears began to subside.

A week or so later, the rest of the story was told me. That Friday afternoon, in a physical breast examination by her doctor, a rather significant lump was found. The doctor was sure, it was a cancer; she should return on Monday for a confirming biopsy. How far had it advanced? The fear of cancer was on her mind as she came to the cup on Sunday.

The next day, the Monday immediately after the communion "event", she reported to the doctor for the biopsy. No lump was there or anywhere! There was nothing to biopsy!

"The Lord shall provide." The clock was ticking, but still no options. I arrived home from work one day; Jeannie was at the door saying, "Here, read this; no, not that; read that little add."

The ad offered an MM (Master of Pastoral Ministry) through the CORPUS program given at Seattle University- all the way across the country from us in Jeannie's home town! That may answer the question, "What next?" I would have my USAF retirement and the GI bill. Finances would be tight, barely sufficient, but enough! This could happen. Let's see what happens!

In a call to Leo Stanford, PhD, Director of CORPUS, I gave him the short version of my story. He was cautiously encouraging, noncommittal. I sent my resume and MS transcripts (graduate with distinction) obtained from the Air Force Institute of Technology. Leo responded with a personal letter, a pile of application forms attached: *much* more encouraging. The forms were routine, except for a required brief life history (with aspirations) and a hang up on the last page. CORPUS included a practicum. Pick one from a list of 50 possibilities.

I didn't like any of them. Boring was my most positive response! Nothing interested me in the slightest! I called Doctor Leo. "I don't like anything on the list. Have you got any other choices?" No. "Well, there is one on the list I don't understand. What is an RCIA?"

He explained. "RCIA stands for Rite of Christian Initiation for Adults. It is a new initiative in the worldwide Catholic Church for the education of converts. You are a convert. This might be of interest to you. You would be teaching and guiding other converts!"

"Sign me up!" The Lord provides.

Everything about CORPUS was right up my alley. Exactly what I wanted, needed, or both: intellectually, psychologically, spiritually. The classes were wonderful: theology, psychology, philosophy, ethics, counseling. Wonderful! The practicum? I soon discovered my identity as a teacher, a catechist. (Not a total surprise. I had considered college teaching several times along the way and my chosen career as a professional manager inherently included a role as practical teacher of my subordinates.) I thrived: learning to witness, learning the arts of catechetics and retreat masters! All of this I would discover and enjoy. But it didn't start that way. Not on the first day!

There were forty or so students in CORPUS that year: one priest from Canada, a brother or two, and approximately an even division of nuns and lay people of all ages. Also, most classes that year would be in the same room of the same old building, with about 50 student desks arranged on the old, oil coated wooden floor. Finally, the main door to the room was at the front right corner, closest to the front right student desk. That position in the class, any class, always had been my preferred spot, ever since grade school.

I was almost late; everyone else was seated. I entered, noticed that my favorite spot was vacant, and sat down. Everyone in the right front quadrant of the class got up and moved as far from me as possible! I checked. Nope, I showered that morning. So my education began.

The curious behavior of the class continued all that week. At breaks, everyone avoided me, did not speak to me in the hall or restroom between classes, sat away from me; shunned me. These are supposed to be Christians! Is this Christian behavior? What gives? They don't even know me! I continued to be myself; asking questions, engaged in dialogue with this or that instructor, answering posed questions.

During the second week, one by one, students began to be polite, more open, even filtering back into the dreaded right front quadrant. In the middle of the third week, a sixty something nun approached me in the hall.

"I owe you an apology," she said. "I am on a student visa in my own country. I used to be an American citizen, but I was so angry with the Vietnam War, I renounced my citizenship and moved to Chile. When I came to my senses, I applied for reinstatement. The State Department said in effect, 'You made your own bed, go lie in it.' I was trapped by my own foolishness. Unfortunately, I had made my bed in Chile. All I knew about the military, any military, was that they came in the night, took people away, and those people were never seen again."

She had landed in Chile in time for the fascist Pinochet regime; where sure enough, people were taken away in the dark by the military, tortured, murdered, and dumped into mass graves.

Leo told the students that they would be joined by a retired Air Force Colonel. He was excited about that; they were not. The nun convinced the class that I was there to spy and to finger victims for kidnapping, torture and murder. They saw me as a thug, a beady- eyed killer. Sweet little old me! It was another great lesson on prejudice. I gave her the Vietnam era standard reply. "No problem." We, the whole class and faculty, soon became and remained good friends throughout the year. Perhaps there was one exception.

The course on ethics was taught by one of the most left wing, radical nuns I had ever met. She was anti-military, knew my background and took every opportunity to pronounce ethical judgments regarding the military. She was in my face. She taught well, however, including her step by step method for ethical analysis: how to attack and decide on difficult ethical questions. I decided to put her to the test. I was going to be a bad ass and find out how strong she was.

We had several papers to write during the semester. The last assignment was to select a difficult topic and come to an ethical judgment. I chose to present an ethical argument for the use of nuclear weapons. If I succeeded, would she stick by her method?

At the end of the semester, my paper came back; A-! She wrote across the front page, "You have used the method correctly and made your case, but personally, I cannot accept your conclusion." She passed the honesty test, but could not accept the consequences of her own method. In my mind, I gave her a B-.

But I had a problem of my own. Once again, time was running out! I interviewed at the chancery office thinking, with my executive background and the MM, I was a shoe in. Wrong! I was yet to learn about church politics; that the same tired specter of prejudice would show again.

The bishop was Hunthousen, a radical "progressive." (Later, he was fired by Pope John Paul II for inappropriate behavior and doctrinal problems and shipped off to oblivion in a remote European monastery- for "retraining," I suppose.) Hunthausen and his staff had roughly the same attitude as my Chilean friend. They hustled me through obviously make believe interviews in each department and showed me the door! I finally turned to my prior profession, aerospace; interviewed first with Boeing, then with Martin-Marietta, who was hiring in town. No fit anywhere. Things were getting desperate.

"The Lord will provide," but He seems to enjoy the cliff hanger! We were down to the last month. Our landlord knew it and he had another tenant in waiting. He was pressuring us to get out, but we had nowhere to go.

I think it was a Tuesday morning. Jeannie and the kids were in the kitchen fixing breakfast. This may sound familiar, but the smell of bacon rolled me out of the bed. As I inserted my left leg in trousers, the phone rang in the living room. This was right at 8:00am. "Get the phone, Al, I can't do it!"

Picture me. At Jeannie's command, I hopped across the living room, one leg in, one leg out, holding up my pants. Jeannie and the kids could see me from the kitchen and were giggling as I processed to the phone. (I also was hurrying to get to a 9:00am class half way across Seattle.) Exasperated, I answered, "Hello?!" Short pause.

Then a voice, not *That Voice,* said, "Can you be on a plane at 11:00 o'clock this morning?"

"Sure," I said. "Where is it going?" Longer pause; mild laughter.

"My secretary took the day off, and I hardly know what I am doing! I guess I should introduce myself. This is Tony Rodriquez, Personnel Director for Federal Electric Corporation at Vandenberg AFB in California. We would like to talk with you. Can you make the plane?"

"Sure. What do I do now?"

"Just go to Sea-Tac Airport. The tickets are already there waiting for you. I'll pick you up in Santa Maria." I did, and he did.

Tony parked me that evening at a motel a few miles from the front gate of Vandenberg AFB. I enjoyed a meal and a couple of drinks at FEC expense and hit the sack. Tony picked me up after breakfast, and delivered me to an interview with David Little. From his bent over physical disability and good natured smile, I immediately recognized this engineer. Nineteen years earlier, a lieutenant training in Missile Range Technology at Patrick AFB, we sat at his desk for the better part of an hour while he discussed his work. After a few prompts, he remembered me as well. We had a long and pleasant interview.

After lunch, I was introduced to Joan Anderson (still a friend, now 27 years later) for a second amiable interview. She was the Department Manager for mathematical analysis. It also was her task to return me to the airport; which she did, including a detour to show me some Santa Maria neighborhoods.

Somewhere along the way between Vandenberg and the first neighborhood, I said, "Joan, there is one thing I don't understand. It felt all day like I was interviewing you and Dave, not the other way around!"

She said, "Don't you know?"

"Don't I know what?"

"We were told to hire you!" (God really *does* provide!)

"Really?! So what happens, now?"

"Go home, sit tight. Tony will call you with an offer from Dave, another from me. Pick the one you like and come on down!" Sure enough, I haggled with Tony by telephone a week later and accepted a position.

Math analysis was intriguing, but long range planning? I was engaged in that for the last four years of active duty. Just change uniforms, so to speak, and keep doing the same kind of work for my beloved Air Force! Besides, Dave offered a higher company rank and more pay!

Why tell you this long winded story? I had not applied for a job with them! Barely knew they existed. They came and got me, anyway!

After the last class, after the last party, after the last farewell and Godspeed, we packed up and headed south. All the way across Washington and Oregon, over and over and over again, the girls on the backseat sang, "Take me where it's warm and dry! Take me where it's warm and dry! Take me where it's warm and dry!" Sure enough, southbound on the coastal highway, right at the Oregon/ California border, it stopped raining, the fog lifted and the sun came out.

In that last couple of weeks at Seattle University, word got around the class that we were going to Santa Maria. A classmate, a forty-ish nun from the Archdiocese of Los Angeles, told me to be sure to join St Louis de Montfort Parish. "It's a wonderful parish, probably the best in the whole Diocese." (A few years later, our auxiliary Bishop referred to the parish as his star of the North.)

Shortly after arrival, we joined up, but did not rush into parish volunteer work. Jeannie was busy checking out grade schools, turning a house into a home and I was determined to make a go of my new quasi-Air Force career in civilian dress. I committed myself exclusively to that for one year. It was a good strategy: by the end of that first year, I was a branch manager, soon to become a Department Manager.

But something was left hanging! All class requirements for the MM were complete, but there was one more task: file a report detailing my post-class accomplishments as a pastoral lay minister in paid or volunteer status. That first year in Santa Maria flew by like a missile launch on steroids. Focused on contract work for the Air Force, I began to procrastinate on the church front! Besides, there was no RCIA at the church where I could put my skills to work.

On a Sunday, I sat down at home after mass to read the parish bulletin. I saw it before I could get comfortable in the easy chair; a tiny little article still burned into my memory. Its title? RCIA! Like Harry on my first day at Antigua, this time, I had ---been had! Honoring my one year set aside, God was still in command; He had set me up. I could guess what was coming next. The article simply said:

"Anyone interested in starting an RCIA program, please attend a Wednesday evening meeting with Father Anthony, in the rectory dining room at 8:30pm."

Wednesday evening, I set out for the church in an emotional split. I felt a great reluctance; along with fascinated anticipation. Exactly where is God going with this?

The centerpiece of the rectory dining room was a long, formal table for twelve. I sat halfway down the table. The pastor, Father Anthony, sat as table commander to my left. There were ten men at table. I chuckled to myself, "There are supposed to be twelve apostles!" I did not recognize any of them, except for the priest.

Father Anthony opened the meeting. "I don't even know what an RCIA is, but the bishop says I have to have one. Does anyone know anything about an RCIA?" For the better part of the next hour, everyone tried to convince him that they knew something. It was all speculation, much in error, or at best inadequate. I did not say a word, not one word after introductions; just watched the show. No one was going to admit ignorance, but they were getting nowhere fast. After a frustrating hour, Father started to close the meeting. I raised my hand.

My first words of the evening were, "It's confession time." Everyone looked at me with shock and dismay, especially Father Anthony. What is he saying? "I have been sand bagging you. We moved here from Seattle last summer, from Seattle University. I studied there for a Masters in Pastoral Ministry. My practicum was the RCIA."

Pointing a finger at me, Father Anthony said, "You're the Director. Meeting adjourned!"

XI. 'E Keeps on Reigning – an Epilogue

I perceive that I am dealt with by superior powers. This is a pleasure, a joy, an existence which I have not procured myself. I speak as a witness on the stand, and tell what I have perceived....

Thoreau

In seven years, we had come from afar in obedience to the Lord's leadings; given in voice or circumstance through his periodic revelation of presence, healing and divine love. We committed ourselves unreservedly through the many twists and turns in our lives. This was no time to stop. The Lord fully prepared us for the RCIA assignment, delivered us to Santa Maria, provided our fiscal needs and this opportunity as well. So Director I would be. In this new "command" we would find great fulfillment by directly promoting the salvation of souls.

Throughout, Jeannie was right there: spouse, friend, counselor, agent of hospitality and protocol "officer." Everything we have done has been a team effort. Naturally, gracefully, she excels as hospitality agent, protocol "officer" and witness in all our joint endeavors. She has her own mission as well: everywhere serving the sick and elderly; serving and teaching youth in churches, on the mean streets of Seattle and in the juvenile detention center at Santa Maria. Together in the Spirit, we have experienced St Paul's list of gifts, from teaching to tongues. These gifts are palpable, real; not given continuously, but present in response to the needs of the moment.

Now you are the body of Christ and individually members of it. And God has appointed in the Church first apostles, second prophets, third teachers: then deeds of power, then gifts of healing, forms of assistance, forms of leadership, various kinds of tongues.

1 Cor 12:27, 28 NRSV

We lived and worked in Santa Maria for seventeen years, from the Summer of '84 to the Spring of '01. We organized and I directed the RCIA team, teaching with a Socratic style, supplementing with guest lectures by priests and presentations by qualified lay ministers. Jeannie promoted hospitality and generally helped in every way. The report of the first three years completed requirements for my Master of Pastoral Ministry degree. Beyond the first six years, I concentrated solely on teaching. Finally, with a separate team, we directed retreats establishing sixteen small faith communities in the parish. The Lord then moved us to Corpus Christi, Texas; from the Mother of God (Santa Maria) to the Body of Christ (Corpus Christi).

Adoration Chapel at Our Lady of Corpus Christi
Corpus Christi, Texas

At Corpus Christi, Jeannie volunteers at Birthright and with her indispensable help, we completed a quarter century in the RCIA, witnessing to thousands; eyeball to eyeball, nose to nose. It has been said, "Save one soul, save your own." Here's hoping!

Still working in the vineyard, soon we are passing, but what about all those who cannot see? Those who are blind to the movements of the Spirit of Unity we see so clearly; who recognize no evidence, hold no understanding, obey nothing but their mortal desires. Most of us start out with such blindness. Many never see. If there is a world of Spirit, why do we not see? Why was I blind for 38 long years? It is so clear, now!

Consider Johari's window, a window with four glass panes. It might be helpful if you drew this. Go get a pencil or pen and a sheet of paper. Draw a large picture of a four pane window. Make it large so that you can write on each pane. On the upper left pane write "I know and I know that I know it." i.e., I know a certain thing, and I know that I know it! Example: I know the English language pretty well, and I know that I know it.

On the upper right pane, write "I don't know and I know that I don't know it" i.e. there are certain things that I don't know and I know that I don't know it. Example: I don't know the German constitution (if they have one) and I know that I don't know it. Now it gets harder.

On the bottom left pane write "I know and I don't know that I know it." Obviously, I can't give you an immediate example because I don't know it. However, as a teacher, I often run into such a situation, because I will say something spontaneously, surprising mostly myself, and upon checking later find that what I said was not only correct, but was exactly what was needed to be said at the time. I suspect all teachers and many others have had this experience.

Now for the really tough one. The bottom right pane! Write "I don't know, and I don't know that I don't know it." i.e., I don't know and I don't even know that the subject exists! Example: As late as 1919, the universe was believed to consist of the solar system surrounded by a scattering of stars and a few "fuzzy" objects. The word "galaxy" and the subject "galaxy" were not dreamed of. Only during the 1920's was it realized that the solar system was an insignificant part of a galaxy and that our galaxy was an insignificant part of an unimaginably large universe of billions of galaxies! "Galaxy" was an unknown, unknown in 1919. Seemingly, there are an infinity of unknown unknowns. That fact alone is worthy of meditation and contemplation. All of us are oblivious to an infinity of real facts!

Putting it another way, nobody has absolute and complete knowledge. Atheists, agnostics, and Christians, all are pilgrims wandering in a strange and mysterious land. We all look for evidence. We all look for truth. We all wander in a dark, uncertain land.

Subject to a multitude of unknown, unknowns, we all are immersed in a life and condition of mystery. Is there really a spiritual, unseen Other? We all operate out of faith of a sort. We answer the question as "Yes, I believe so"; or "No, I don't" or "I don't know." And many of us vacillate. Or do we live in a Flip Wilson world where "What you see is what you get!" We have an additional problem.

In the midst of mystery, we also suffer the cultural effects of a philosophical plague, a quartet of "-isms": materialism, positivism, rationalism, and relativism. As paradigms, these "-isms" and others infect us all: atheists, agnostics and religious, alike. None of us are totally immune to paradigms: as the great wall of Antigua blocked the air of night, these paradigms block perception of Spiritual light.

(As a freshman in an engineering orientation class, I was taught, "If you find yourself in an argument, stop; define your terms. Most disagreements are over semantics, not facts." So let's be absolutely clear.)

Definition of Paradigm: A model or pattern (Mirriam-Webster); or archetype (Webster's Ninth New Collegiate Dictionary). As used here, a paradigm is a set of ideas (thought patterns), half conscious assumptions, which people have learned and which define "conventional wisdom" about nature and life. Paradigms act as mental filters, limiting the way we think, providing a set of boundary conditions which are perceived, but are often unreal.

I beg you to make this definition your own. Meditate on it if necessary before you continue. Understanding of paradigm-effects on thought is critical to what follows.

Those four "-isms", mentioned above, were born in the 18th century, culturally matured in the 19th and became endemic in the 20th century; they are assumptions deeply embedded in our minds today. Unnoticed, they limit the way we think, placing boundaries that may not be real. They generate concerns about evidence for Spiritual existence and understanding in Faith. All of us grapple with this question:

What evidence is available to lend credence to Christian Faith?

For 38 years, my answer was "none." Like many, I could not think beyond the boundaries imposed by those subconscious paradigms. Nor, un-churched as I was, did I know there were subjects and sources that could help: such as Saint Thomas's classical proofs--- he and a legion of other sources were for me, Johari's unknown, unknowns. I knew of no hard evidence.

The first boundary of thought we impose on ourselves is to assume that physical matter is the fundamental reality (Materialism: the theory that physical matter is the only or fundamental reality. All being, processes and phenomena can be explained as manifestations or results of matter.) Nearly everyone operates on the unconscious assumption that perceptible matter is the fundamental reality. We need to examine that assumption (that paradigm.)

Einstein postulated, and experiments (including the atomic and hydrogen bombs) have shown that matter is a form of energy. Matter transforms to energy in atomic reactions and energy transforms to matter in the explosive pressure cookers of the cosmos. It is all energy in one form or another. Seen any energy lately? Not the effects of energy, but energy, itself? I think not!

Black holes in space are accepted as reality, too, but no one has, or can see one. All that can be discerned are the effects of the unseen black hole.

Yet, while few deny unseen energy or black holes as reality, many question the reality of unseen Spirit. Let's be fair! If unseen energy and black holes are detected by their effects, why not seek the reality of Spirit by its (His?) effects?!

Along with materialism, the companion paradigm boundary we impose on thought is to expect all knowledge of reality eventually to be verified by empirical science, (positivism: the theory that theology and metaphysics are earlier imperfect modes of knowledge; that positive knowledge is based on natural phenomena, their properties and relations as verified by the empirical sciences.)

Accepting these two paradigms and their associated thought boundaries together, evidence of unseen Spirit, or unseen anything else, must be derived from scientific study of time, matter and energy (so called natural phenomena.) We never say that, but that is the net result of our paradigm bound thinking.

Accepting those boundaries without thinking it through, we finesse all possibilities for discerning evidence of an unseen and un-seeable creator (dwelling outside of time, space, and matter); dwelling instead, solely on evidence from the created. Some even protest the use of the words "creator" and "created" as meaningless terms within the boundaries imposed by those paradigms.

Our understanding becomes even more limited. Restrained by positivism, we assume real knowledge will be verified by scientific methods, methods which require observable and repeatable evidence so that other scientists can repeat the same experiments and arrive at the same conclusions; a consensus regarding some aspect of reality. That approach is quite successful in advancing our understanding of the physical (created) world, but empirical science is not up to the search for a spiritual (creator) world. (Empirical: capable of being verified or disproven by observation or experiment.) Who can "observe or experiment" on spirit? Who can verify or disprove a world of spirit with observable and repeatable experimentation?

Properly understood, there is evidence for the spiritual world of Christian Faith; found in anecdotal accounts of non-repeatable individual observation and experience. But we tend to dismiss this type of evidence; it is outside of our paradigm boundaries.

Personal, non-repeatable experiences rendered in anecdotal accounts are evidence; given credence as they correlate with many other individual stories. Our own stories are not strange and unique experiences; our anecdotes are similar to many others as we learn where to look. Every anecdote is like a statistical data point. Collect enough of them and common patterns of experience emerge. Conclusions about the reality of God shift from subjective hope toward objective clarity. There are countless mutually correlating anecdotes of "God-effects" written and spoken since Abraham, more than 4,000 years ago. They are in Scripture, in the writings of Saints, in works of the Church and even in the writings of some scientists.

Should you dismiss religious sources out of hand, there are a number of other sources, (though I encourage you always to study Christian Scripture. It was written by real people living in their own time, reporting anecdotally what they knew directly, or heard about.) If you can find it, you should read philosopher/ psychologist William James, PhD's Varieties of Religious Experience, first published in 1902 and reprinted in 1904.

James presents around 500 pages of anecdotes, correlations and analyses base on numerous accounts he collected in the late 19th century. Or read psychologist Karl Jung, PhD's discussions in various works regarding "synchronicity" which he defined as "meaningful coincidence." The old doctor must have had his tongue firmly in his cheek when he coined that definition; it sounds like an oxymoron.

But he was referring to "coincidental" events that statistically are impossible to expect, but do occur and have specific invitational and actionable meaning for one or more present individuals; implying an unseen, communicating Mind at work behind such events. There are other works available, including some by theoretical physicists (cosmologists.) There are even suggestions in some scientific quarters that the fundamental reality may not be matter, but the unseen life principle i.e. spirit! I leave the search for sources of evidence to the committed reader. And who knows what you might find that has escaped our attention. There is so much out there! The search is half the fun of discovery. The trip is half the fun of getting there.

On the other hand, those committed to the paradigms of materialism and positivism, secure in their paradigm boundaries, may never see all there is to see.

Having been booted over the evidence hurdle by The Voice while in Antigua, the next issue was resolved almost simultaneously. Relationship proved to be the best evidence of all!

The next question is... what must be understood to develop a strong belief in Christian Faith? It's a trick question, but first there's rationalism to contend with. Rationalism suggests that we can think our way to truth about religion, about God. As a paradigm, this approach is fraught with danger. It unconsciously devalues or ignores Revelation and experience, focusing on logic. "I can think my way to the truth." Logic and reason are necessary, but not sufficient! And just how logical is our reasoning, anyway?

It makes sense to apply logic and decide; thus and so is true about things in the physical world. And so, on the basis of confirmed evidence, we "understand" the physical world to the extent of current knowledge and then "believe" what we have found to be true, at least until we find contrary empirical evidence.

But in the search for a Spiritual world, we are looking for a Person or Persons, not some thing! (Person: a rational being: perfectly subsistent, master of its own acts, and incommunicable. A Catholic Dictionary, Donald Attwater, ed.)

We look for a Rational Being. If we try truly to understand anything about that Being so that we can believe in Him, we probably won't make it. I am routinely perplexed by my own spouse. How will I understand anything about The Infinite One?

Who are you to put God to the test today, and to set yourselves up in the place of God in human affairs? You cannot plumb the depths of the human heart or understand the workings of the human mind; how do you expect to search out God, who made all these things, and find out his mind or comprehend his thought? Therefore, while we wait for his deliverance, let us call upon Him to help us, and he will hear our voice, if it pleases Him.
Judith 8: 12, 14, 17 NRSV

In my own hard headed case, I spent years trying to figure out a logical rationale that would lead to belief. I was in the position "Because I don't understand, I can't believe." I did not know that was a classic dilemma! It is no surprise that I did not find Anyone!

Saint Anselm (1033-1109) affirms,

"Nor do I seek to understand that I may believe, but I believe that I may understand. For this too, I believe, that unless I first believe, I shall not understand."

He could have said, go to the source. Go direct. Obtain the relationship that is offered; not just ideas or concepts, but relationship!

I was frozen in my dilemma, could not get to God, so The Voice came to me! He broke the ice with a subtle proposition of relationship. I soon realized that knowledge, wisdom and understanding flow from God through relationship, not only or first from my own mental gymnastics! Christian Scripture even tells us how to gain relationship. We have a road map.

So I say unto you, ask and it will be given you, search, and you will find, knock and the door will be opened for you. For everyone who asks receives, and everyone who searches finds, and for everyone who knocks, the door will be opened.

Lk 11: 9,10 NRSV

"Ask and it will be given...." Belief (faith) cannot be grasped; it is a gift asked for and received; received at a time and manner not of your choosing. Knowledge, wisdom and understanding take years of living in relationship with God and other Christian travelers (it's about relationship with them, too!) The gift is promised! Give it a shot! Pray! Ask!

The Voice had to go so far as to kick start me, suggesting, "Pretend to believe...." as sufficient to begin a relationship. Still, I did ask years earlier in the midst of a mid-Alaskan winter, even in my unbelief. I asked and belief was given (Five years later!) I searched and little by little found. I knocked and the door almost fell open! Ask! Then, be open, vigilant and patient.

We get locked up on our ideas without really thinking it through. That is how paradigms work. One example will suffice.

John was giving his pitch to a new RCIA group. He started talking about angels, the devil, and evil spirits. Linda shot out of her chair. "There's no such thing as a spiritual world. No such thing as angels, or the devil or evil spirits. Superstition! We know better, now!" (Positivism? Rationalism? Both?) It started an emotional battle between the two. After a few minutes it was getting out of control; I had to step in.

"Linda, do you believe in God?" She did. "And God is Spirit?" She agreed. "Good, so we have a spiritual world populated by at least one Spirit. And where are your parents?" She hoped they were in heaven. "Good! Now we have a spirit world populated by at least three. What about your other ancestors, and those of everyone else, here?" Heaven was getting crowded! "And maybe if there are many of these spirits there, there might be other kinds of spirits, as well? Some better than others? Maybe, even some were rebellious and got thrown out? And one of them might be the worst of all"? Linda sat down.

No proof was given or intended, but she had to consider beyond the boundaries of her paradigms, learned in secular Santa Barbara; to be open beyond the boundaries of positivism. In fairness, twenty odd years later Linda is still a dear friend; a hard charging Christian woman teaching at a Catholic High School. She refers to young secular lights as "rebels without a clue!"

Do not get hung up on preconceptions. Ask in prayer and believe, even if under pretense. It is as Saint Anselm proposed. "…I believe, that I might understand." At the end of his life research psychologist Karl Jung was asked if he believed in God. With a mischievous grin he said, "No." Pausing for effect he then said, "I don't believe in Him, I know Him." That is relationship!

I hear and I forget

I see and I remember

I do and I understand

In this case, the do-ing is to ask, seek, knock and persevere. And personally, I would recommend that you seek within the Roman Catholic Church, the only two thousand year old church established by Jesus and his Apostles in the flesh. That church is where He sent me!

Finally, there is the question of obedience! Must you lose control of your life?

This is one problem I never had. Perhaps it was my military experience. I was sitting in our dining room at table one evening, chatting with Ronda Chervin, a noted Catholic writer who has published more than 50 books. It was after dinner; Jeannie, with other guests, had retreated to the library. Somehow we got around to the subject of obedience. "It's curious, Ronda. In the Air Force, nobody talked about obedience, but everybody obeyed. In _____ (a religious society of our mutual acquaintance), everybody talks about obedience, but nobody obeys!" She pondered that for maybe 10 or 15 seconds and sadly agreed.

In California we often attend the annual Southern California Renewal Conference (SCRC) at Anaheim. The conference is staged in a moderate size sports dome filled with Charismatic (Pentecostal) Christians, mostly Catholics. Each year, they gather 6 to 12 thousand strong, to hear talks on many spiritual subjects and celebrate mass together.

One particular year, Father Bob Lussier was giving his first talk. There were 300 people crowded into a ballroom at the adjacent Hilton. We sat in the extreme back right corner of the packed room. From there, we could see the entire audience. After the speaker introduction, Father Bob launched into his talk. Maybe ten minutes into the talk he turned to the topic of "obedience." Fifteen people (I could see them all and counted) stood bolt upright, quickly gathered their belongings and stalked out. On the lockjaw grim faces of the nearer escapees, anger was evident.

> *"Satan can even clothe himself in a cloak of humility, but he does not know how to wear the cloak of obedience."*
> *St. Faustina's Diary*

Father Bob paused; he and the rest of the crowd watched the out-rushing exodus in amazement. When they had cleared the room, he said, "There, that is exactly what I am talking about, the aversion to obedience, even in the Church." (At the end of his talk, he received a standing ovation!)

The point? To some people, obedience is a four letter word. "I have rights and I am free. No one can tell me what to do!" Their attitude smacks of relativism. "Your truth may not be my truth and you have no right to impose your truth on me." They recognize no absolutes, no call to obedience. Truth is whatever they choose it to be. It amounts to intellectual anarchy. Effectively, they act as their own authority in all matters; they are their own god.

Relativism is becoming pervasive in the secular culture; it spills over into many Church congregations. Some pick and choose what they like, reinterpret as they like, and leave the rest for someone else. They question, avoid, or outright reject appropriate ecclesial authority. It seems irrational, but like Linda, like all of us; often, folks get locked up on a concept or mode without really thinking it through- relativism is another paradigm!

Relationship, any relationship, requires some form and extent of obedience to the needs and desires of another. Nowhere in Scripture is it written, "Come along and do as you please!"

They who have my commandments and keep them are those who love me; and those who love me will be loved by my Father, and I will love them and reveal myself to them.
John 14:21 NRSV

We find these words of Christ to be conditions that advance real spiritual relationship with the Spirit of Unity. Not suggestions, but commandments. Not pick one, but keep them. Not intellectual interest in them, but love expressed through them. Not know about God, but Himself revealed! For us, information was not enough. We wanted relationship.

Obedience! Must you lose control of your life? The short answer is no. Here is the long answer:

...there is another martyrdom; the martyrdom of love. Here God keeps his servants and handmaids in this present life so that they may labor for him, and He makes them both martyrs and confessors. Yield yourself fully to God, and you will find out! Divine love takes its sword to the hidden recesses of our inmost soul and divides us from ourselves: from the moment when we commit ourselves unreservedly to God, until our last breath. I am speaking, of course, of great-souled individuals who keep nothing back for themselves, but instead are faithful in love. Our Lord does not intend this martyrdom for those who are weak in love and perseverance. Such people he lets continue on their mediocre way, so that they will not be lost to him; he never does violence to our free will.

Saint Jane Frances de Chantal, religious

Saint Jane gives us a couple of options; general obedience or specific (heroic) obedience. And, of course, by obedience is meant obedience to the will of God. Carefully reread-even meditate on Saint Jane's comments, then think of it this way. God has a general will for all of us, resident in the moral and spiritual life commanded by Christ and proposed by Scripture, the Apostles and the Saints; i.e., the Scripture, teachings, authority (the Magisterium) and Tradition of the Roman Catholic Church, which Jesus founded in his Apostles. (The mission of the Catholic Church is to protect and promulgate the teachings of Jesus Christ and his Apostles –not to change, adapt, or "modernize" them!) The study and application of His general will is a lifelong effort.

If we are open to His specific will meant for our self and our self alone, look out! As my pastor put it in a recent homily, "If he finds you open (obedient), he will move in and take over!" Yes, He will (!), not to produce of you a robot, but to invite a junior associate to His work.

If anything is certain about the will of God, it is that He wills to honor our freedom of will, the gift He gave us from the beginning. Free will makes us persons rather than high class animals. To take away our freedom of will is to destroy our personhood, zenith of his creation. "The glory of God is man, fully alive!" (Irenaus) God will not destroy His own glory.

At no time, even when The Voice was clearly heard, was an order given. Every time, vocal or circumstantial; an option was implied, suggested, offered, preferred, even urged, but never ordered. I had complete control of my will. The closest He ever got to an order, was saying "...I want you to...," knowing that the most difficult occasion for obedience I would ever face was the separation from my beloved Air Force. Only with my own free choice to obey, did he "...divide me from myself," my beloved Air Force. As Saint Jane put it,

Yield yourself fully to God, and you will find out! Divine love takes its sword to the hidden recesses of our inmost soul and divides us from ourselves: from the moment when we commit ourselves unreservedly to God, until our last breath.

The key word there is unreservedly, the secret of the saints. The question is not obedience, but to what extent are we willing to obey? That brings us back to St Jane, again.

I am speaking, of course, of great-souled individuals who keep nothing back for themselves, but instead are faithful in love. Our Lord does not intend this martyrdom for those who are weak in love and perseverance. Such people he lets continue on their mediocre way, so that they will not be lost to him; he never does violence to our free will.

Meditate on the words of St Jane. We all make the choice explicitly or implicitly: pick one. In the context of our own gifts and circumstance, all of us will be mediocre, "weak in love and perseverance;" or move toward strength "in love and perseverance," even to "heroic obedience," the avenue of the saints. We have never lost our free will, but we have offered our wills freely in gratitude and joyous anticipation. First believe, then obey, then understand.

To know and not to do, is not yet to know.

Psalm 40

I waited patiently for the Lord;
he inclined to me and heard my cry.
He drew me up from the desolate pit,
out of the miry bog,
and set my feet upon a rock,
making my steps secure.
He put a new song in my mouth,
a song of praise to our God.
Many will see and fear,
and put their trust in the Lord.
You have multiplied, O Lord, my God,
your wondrous deeds
and your thoughts toward us;
none can compare with you.
Were I to proclaim and tell of them,
they would be more than can be counted.
I delight to do your will, O my God;
your law is within my heart.
I have told the glad news of deliverance
in the great congregation;
see, I have not restrained my lips,
as you know, O Lord.
I have not hidden your saving help within my heart,
I have spoken of your faithfulness and your salvation;
I have not concealed your steadfast love
and your faithfulness from the great congregation.
But may all who seek you
rejoice and be glad in you;
may those who love your salvation say continually,
"Great is the Lord!"
As for me, I am poor and needy,
but the Lord takes thought for me.
You are my help and my deliverer;
do not delay, O my God.
Verses 1-3, 5, 8-10, 16,17 NRSV

Brothers and Sisters, Do Not Be Afraid

To welcome Christ and accept his power. Do Not Be Afraid.

Christ knows "what is in man." He alone knows it.

So often today man does not know what is within him,

In the depths of his mind and heart.

So often he is uncertain about the meaning of life on this earth.

He is assailed by doubt, a doubt that turns into despair.

We ask you therefore, we beg you with humility and trust,

Let Christ speak to man.

He alone has words of life, yes, of eternal life.

Blessed Pope John Paul II
From his initial homily as pope, October 22, 1978